QUILTING

MOYRA McNEILL

octopus

812909

ENLARGING A DESIGN

To make the most of the projects in this book you will need to be able to enlarge a design to the correct size. The designs are printed on grids – the smallest squares of which are equivalent to one centimetre. In order to enlarge them to scale you will need graph paper ruled in one-centimetre squares. (Alternatively, draw up your own grid.) You will also need a ruler and felt-tipped pen. Copy the design, positioning each part within the centimetre square corresponding to the small square in which it falls on the printed page.

In a few cases, the amount of enlargement required is very slight, and so, for convenience, we have simply reduced the size of the design without a grid. In these cases the size of the completed design is not vital to the success of the project, and we have simply provided the outside measurements as a guide.

NOTES FOR AMERICAN READERS

Certain words and terms used in this book may not be familiar to American readers. So that American readers may fully understand the information and instructions, the American equivalents have been given in brackets [] throughout.

**First published 1980 by
Octopus Books Limited
59 Grosvenor Street
London W1**

© 1980 Octopus Books Limited
ISBN 0 7064 1345 8
D.L. TO - 655-80

Printed in Spain by
Artes Graficas, Toledo

CONTENTS

HISTORY

It is difficult to trace really old samples of many textiles, since by their very nature they are extremely perishable. Either they have been destroyed through normal wear and tear, or stored in unsuitable conditions such as damp, in which they have badly deteriorated. Just for this reason it is impossible to know when quilting began. It seems such a common sense idea to sandwich fabrics together to make warmer clothes or coverings than one layer would provide, that it cannot have taken human beings long to discover it, but we have no early examples extant. The nearest we can get is a piece of soft sculpture of a swan made in felt and stuffed with deer hair, which may have been one of four figures on a canopy of a grave, or ceremonial carriage. The swan is about 2,300 years old and was one of the treasures from a frozen tomb in Siberia, but looks modern and shows a high degree of skill in modelling fabric.

In Greek and Roman sculpture, borders and patterns are shown in relief on clothing, but are they woven, embroidered or quilted? Rather than speculating or guessing, we must satisfy ourselves with what actually remains, and portraits are a good place to start.

Opposite: Portrait of a man *by Titian, showing a richly quilted sleeve of blue silk.*

Right: This detail shows a border section of a mid 18th-century New Hampshire quilt. The top is made of indigo-dyed, glazed calamanco. It is backed with homespun and padded with sheep's fleece. The border is beautifully quilted in a bold curling leaf pattern and diagonal lines. The centre of the quilt is worked in a diamond pattern.

Left: A magnificent example of 19th-century horse armour from the Sudan. The thick padding is formed by many layers of locally woven cloth stitched together. The top is decorated with brightly coloured patchwork triangles in black, red, yellow and blue. The patchwork pieces have been applied to the top layer of padding and the whole design enriched with parallel lines of stitching.

Opposite: This quilt was made in 1933 by Miss Edwards of Glamorgan, Wales, and is a very fine example of her work. It was used as a working example and displayed during her quilting demonstrations. The top is of mercerized poplin and the padding is wool. The spiral design used in the central diamond shape and repeated in the surrounding borders was part of the repertoire of Welsh quilters, while the central rose pattern was Miss Edwards' own design. The very detailed pattern shows off the quilting to full effect.

EXAMPLES IN ART

In the National Gallery in London there is a portrait by Titian of a man wearing a full quilted sleeve, thought to be possibly a self-portrait and dating from the early 1500s. Titian's painting skill tells at once that the blue sleeve is richly padded all over, is clearly made of silk, and is quilted in widely spaced lines, sewn down occasionally in between and gathered into a broad cuff, similarly quilted. In a 15th-century French manuscript there is an illustration of a lady dressed in green. She is shown seated in a corner, listening to Bishop Arundel speaking. Her clothing looks padded, has a silky sheen and is indented in horizontal bands but the scale is too small to indicate any more. In the chilly buildings of that time, quilting would have been an eminently practical way of keeping warm.

MILITARY USES

It is certain that padded jerkins or waistcoats [vests] were worn under armour to prevent it chafing, and these were quilted in simple bands. Such a garment, reputed to belong to the Black Prince, was on show in Canterbury cathedral for many years, though it has now been replaced with a copy. The Spanish Cortés and Pizarro expeditions to the Americas to bring back gold, clothed some foot soldiers in 'poor man's armour', which was a quilted cotton doublet called a 'jack'. Quilted cotton for defensive armour was found preferable to metal in these expeditions – 'the moisture not being suitable for armour' – and every soldier in the 1573 de Soto enterprise to Florida was issued with it. Thickly padded garments were also a cheap and practical alternative to the heavy and cumbersome chain-mail, as well as an effective protection against arrows.

QUILTING IN FASHIONABLE DRESS

Up to this time quilted clothing was a matter of utility rather than decoration and not until 100 years later did both English and Italian quilting come into fashion for both clothing and furnishings. In the time of James I and Charles I, men wore suits of English quilted satin, consisting of breeches and a doublet with sleeves. If we can judge by the amount of quilting remaining from the 1700s it would seem that everyone had quilted clothing – men, women and children.

One of the most typical garments of this period is the gentleman's white linen waistcoat, which was always richly decorated down the front where it showed, but made with a plain back, sometimes laced to ensure a snug fit. The pattern of decoration was based on simplified bold flower and leaf shapes totally covered in embroidery, combining Italian quilting, surface stitchery and drawn fabric stitches. The front fly fastening had small buttons from neck to near hem, all hand worked, but usually only half were fastened, the rest being entirely for decoration. Pocket flaps were essential on either side, but did not always have a pocket underneath.

The typical quilted lady's garment of this period is the 'underskirt' visible from waist to hem under the robe, which was usually made of a rich woven fabric with a sack-back and sometimes supported with hoops. The underskirt itself was very voluminous and quilted all over, even where it did not show; the patterns were bold stylized floral shapes near the hem, becoming geometric fillings in the upper part. The whole was of fine silk with a light layer of padding and was English quilted in running stitch, giving a rich, handsome effect. A letter to the *Spectator* of 11 October 1714, gives a human insight . . .

'I have a couple of nieces under my direction who so often run gadding abroad that I don't know where to have them. Their dress, their tea and their visits take up all their time and they go to bed as tired with doing nothing as I am after quilting a whole under petticoat' . . . .

Children and particularly babies were not forgotten, and babies' caps, some very small, are typical of the 1700s. The caps were frequently richly decorated with Italian quilting and other techniques, making a bumpy surface which cannot have been comfortable for the child.

Quilted clothes were fashionable throughout western Europe at this time.

THE QUILTED COVERLET

The other great source of historical quilting is, of course, the coverlet – not always made for warmth but often for pure decoration. One of the oldest and most attractive quilts ever made comes from Sicily. It was made in about 1400 and was designed for a bed 2.5 m (8 ft) long and similarly wide; in a series of 'frames' about 75 cm (30 in) by 95 cm (38 in) the story of Tristram, who was a 'superman' of medieval romance, is told, very much in the manner of strip cartoons today, as each scene contains an explanatory sentence between the battling figures in armour. The fabric used was a heavy off-white linen in two layers and the figures were outlined in brown back stitch before being trapunto quilted. However, there is some mystery as to how this was done, as there is no sign of a hole or a slit for the padding to be inserted from the wrong side. Borders of formalized leaves and flowers divide the scenes and these are worked in natural-coloured thread and also padded. The Tristram quilt is in the Victoria and Albert museum in London, but a similar one is in the Bargello in Florence. Another surviving example from the same workshop is called the Pianetti quilt.

Although inventories of the 1500s indicate that many coverlets existed, they were nearly all in forms of embroidery other than quilting; but quilted coverlets reappear from the late 1600s throughout the 1700s. There were two distinct styles; in one kind the fabrics were off-white linen and a tightly twisted silk thread was used to form geometric patterns in back-stitched flat quilting, covering the whole area. The thread was gently coloured, often yellow, and being twisted and thick gave the lines of stitchery a bead-like quality. Pillows, not intended to be slept on, but for decoration only, were also made to match the coverlets and looked very handsome against the wood of a four poster bed. The other style was more flamboyant: coverlets were made of satin or silk with a fine linen backing and also flat quilted, after which large baskets and bunches of flowers were embroidered in the corners and the middle. Popular flower designs included the rose, carnation and tulip – then very expensive. They were worked in colourful silk threads in long and short stitch, sometimes with areas of metal thread on the baskets, creating a most sumptuous effect; these also had matching pillows.

THE AMERICAN TRADITION

Quilting was taken to America by English colonists. In Philadelphia, in a reconstructed house of Benjamin Franklin's era, there is on display a bed with a deeply quilted coverlet of calamanco.

This was a glazed woollen fabric usually dyed with dark colours and, though less grand than its European counterparts, it was both practical and effective.

The making of quilts was an important part of domestic life in Early America, and their design and construction show great originality and skill. Very briefly, the most typical quilts were either 'pieced' or applied or a mixture of both, making the top side bright with colourful motifs arranged in an overall pattern. The whole was then English quilted in bold running stitch. Quite often this has no relation to the top side pattern, and can only be seen to

full effect on the underside. Many patterns for the quilt tops were taken from everyday objects, but historical events also gave their names to designs. The quilting was often done by groups of women working together – an occasion dubbed a 'quilting bee', which also served as an opportunity for socializing.

QUILT MAKING IN WALES

It was a social need that reawakened the art of quilting in the 1930s in South Wales; it was always an area where quilt making was traditional, and sewing women used to be employed as they were in earlier centuries, to go from house to house for two or three weeks at a time to do any sewing that was wanted, including quilting. The fillings were of washed fleece which children were allowed to play with to tease it out, before it was laid in carefully as the padding for English quilted bedspreads. To help the morale of women in the depressed areas of South Wales in the 1930s, a revival of quilting was sponsored under the guidance of a Miss Edwards, and many excellent quilts resulted.

Durham is also known for its quilting tradition; as in Wales, simple template shapes including leaves, feathers and circles were combined to build up intricate overall patterns. These are worked in bold running stitches to form reversible quilts, often with a different colour each side.

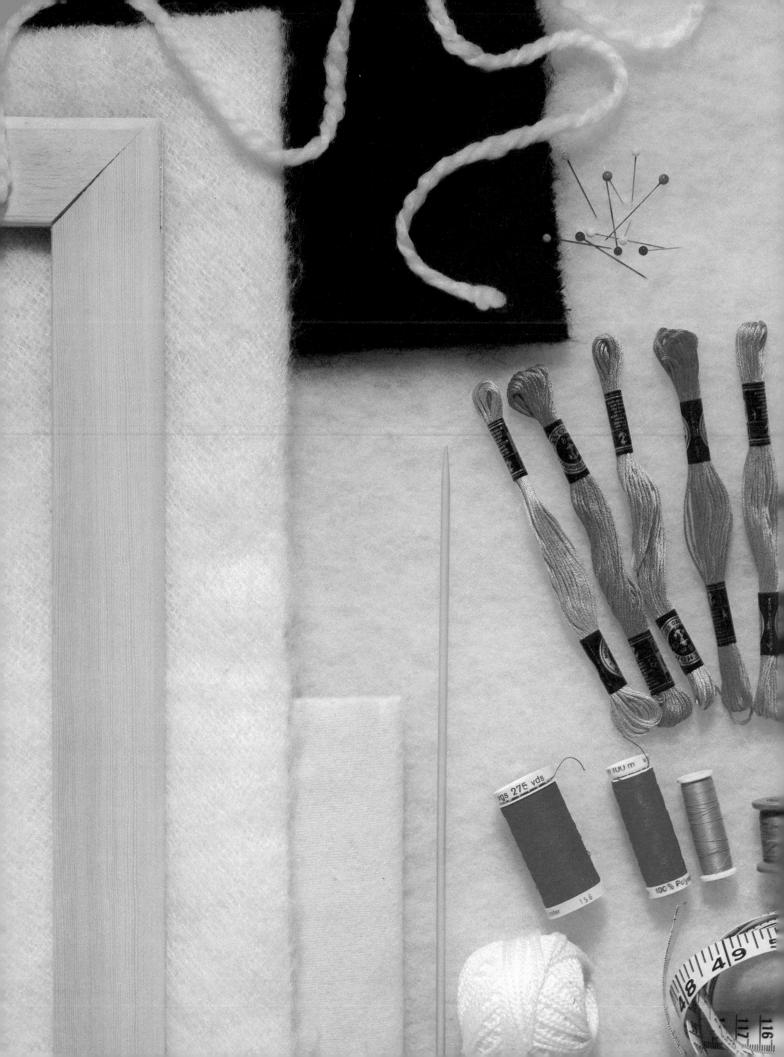

MATERIALS

In past years it used to be considered that only certain fabrics were appropriate to some techniques of decorative needlework. Linen or lawn was usually chosen for smocking, satin or pure silk for quilting, dress cotton for patchwork and even weave linen for counted thread embroidery, for example. Nowadays, the old 'traditional' fabrics are often difficult to obtain or have gone out of manufacture altogether, and instead a choice has to be made from dress and furnishing fabrics made from all sorts of fibres, which can be very bewildering.

CHOOSING THE BEST FABRIC

In many forms of quilting the fabric is required to stretch over padding, so it must have some elasticity or it will pucker. This fabric characteristic can either be due to the weave or construction of the fabric, or to the individual fibres having an inherent stretchiness.

Knitted fabrics, often marketed under the general title of 'jersey', are ideal for very padded surfaces, because the loops of the knitting will move further apart than the unders and overs of the warp and weft of a plain woven fabric. Single jersey is sometimes unstable for fashion use, because of its excessively stretchy qualities. However it is excellent for very highly padded surfaces, and can be obtained in synthetic fibres, cotton or wool. Double jersey has a more complicated interlock knitted structure to make it more stable for clothing, and therefore it is not quite so stretchy; it can be obtained in woollen and synthetic fibres.

Satin may be constructed in a variety of ways but the feature of its construction is long 'floats' of warp over weft. In very general terms the better the quality of satin – that is, the finer and closer the weave, the less suitable it is for tightly padded quilting, because the fabric is more rigid; such satins are known as duchess satin or double satin.

Crepe can be made in several ways but the most useful for quilting are those crepes which are constructed of very hard twist yarns, making them crinkle, or those with special crepe weaves, which have a random weave structure, giving a fluid surface. A crepe effect can be embossed or printed onto the surface of a fabric. This type is suitable for anything except flat quilting, or a very flat padded English quilting.

Felt is an unusual fabric because there is no basic 'weave'; it is made of woollen fibres compressed under heat and moisture, so that they congeal. Felt of the weight sold for craftwork will stretch well, but will shrink with washing, so it is not suitable for practical items. One point to watch when selecting felt is to avoid the very flimsy varieties as any pressure, like padding, can cause the fabric to split away from the stitching.

Wool comes in several distinctive kinds, varying with the different breeds of sheep. The quality it has that is most useful for fabrics to be quilted is a crimp or permanent wave in the fibre that gives it elasticity. Therefore many woollen fabrics are suitable for quilting, including crepe, fine flannels, hopsack, jersey, georgette and Viyella, which is a wool and cotton mixture.

Pure silk of the finest quality is made from the filament unwound from the cocoon of the cultivated silk worm. It is resilient and has a lustrous, rich texture. The more finely woven silk fabrics often have the most drapable qualities which make them resilient over paddings. These include jap silk [China silk], georgette, and surah. Wild [raw] silk is what its name suggests, silk from wild silk worms, which, because of its irregular nature, is often woven into bolder fabrics which have beautiful slub-marked surfaces. It is much stiffer in character than the finely woven fabrics and therefore only suitable for the flatter forms of quilting.

Suede or leather can be readily quilted because, being animal skins, they are naturally flexible. However the thinner leathers, such as glove leather, are the most suitable. The stitching will be easier if a small gloving needle is used for hand work and a machine leather needle for machine sewing.

Imitation suede is now on the market and has the benefit of being washable. It is perfectly suitable for all but the most highly padded quilting.

As general advice, when selecting fabrics for quilting, look for fabrics with a fluid, draping quality for the most padded kinds of quilting, and choose those with a firmer feel for flat quilting or where less padding is involved.

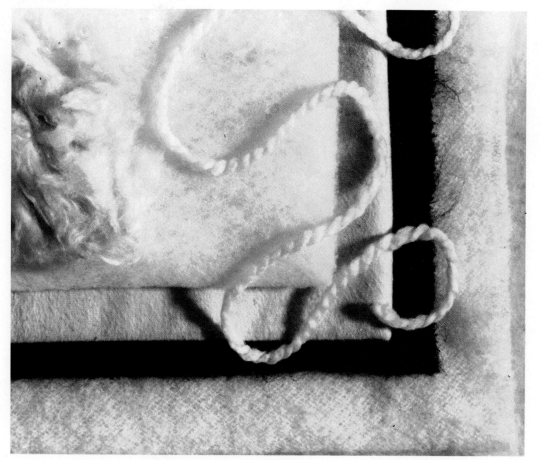

The wadding [padding] with the fleece-like appearance is kapok – an ideal material for trapunto (stuffed) quilting. The quilting wool is used for Italian (corded) quilting, while the other types of wadding [padding] shown are all suitable for the English and appliqué techniques.

WADDINGS [PADDINGS]

The purpose of wadding [padding] in clothing or quilts is to form an insulation between the body and the air outside, in order to make a warm garment or bed covering; if the insulation can be open enough to retain air, the heat retention will be all the better. Nowadays there are many kinds of wadding, but their availability can vary from area to area; also, new types are introduced from time to time, while older ones are withdrawn. The following descriptions are of waddings on the market at the time of writing, but you may find new – and possibly better – varieties becoming available later. Many waddings sold today are synthetic, which means that their fibres are made from chemicals.

Synthetic waddings are not woven or knitted but constructed by laying the fibres side by side, an effect resembling carded fleece. This makes a light, open filling, which has the great benefit of being drip-dry, as the fibres do not retain moisture as wool or cotton fibres do.

Courtelle (acrylic) wadding is usually sold in a 1.2 cm ($\frac{1}{2}$ in) thickness. The acrylic fibre used was developed in the search for a wool substitute; it may be layered to form a thicker wadding if required.

Tricel (cellulose triacetate) wadding is about 2.5 cm (1 in) thick and is folded with a paper-like surface on the outside. Open out this wadding and place the papery side next to the back or wrong side of the quilting with the fluffy side uppermost. Cellulose triacetate is a very distant cousin of rayon, which was developed in the search for an alternative to pure silk. It is a little more dense and compact than other synthetic waddings.

Terylene (polyester) wadding [Dacron] is sold in a variety of thicknesses up to 7 cm ($2\frac{3}{4}$ in) and is a very bouncy wadding. Polyester fibres are closely related to nylon.

Never iron synthetic waddings or they will flatten permanently. Obviously, synthetic waddings are particularly suitable for any washable items, as they launder well; but natural waddings are available which may serve the purpose as well, or even better.

The traditional wadding is **sheep's fleece**. The fleece is first gently washed, then either carded – which both cleans it and organizes it into parallel fibres – or teased out by hand. The wool is then arranged on the backing, piece by piece, so that all the fibres lie in the same direction.

Another pure wool wadding is **domette**. This has a very open knitted structure with a fluffy brushed surface; it has the quality of warmth with little bulk, so is particularly suitable for quilting fashion clothing.

There is also a form of **cotton domette** which is woven and resembles flannelette; although primarily an interlining, it is useful for a thin, flat quilted effect.

Cotton wadding was widely used before the synthetics appeared. It has the same papery surface as Tricel and should be treated in the same way. It is a rather solid wadding and does not wash well, so the synthetic alternatives are generally preferable.

Old blankets or coats were used in the past as an economic recycling of fabric in quilts. In a similar way one or more layers of felt may be used as a wadding.

LININGS/BACKINGS

In general it is best to choose a firm backing both for padded quilting and trapunto quilting, or the quilted effect may be more pronounced on the wrong side than the right! Italian (corded) quilting requires a more giving fabric, or threading the wool through the parallel channels can be made very difficult. Although muslin is often recommended as a backing for this form of quilting, the muslin now available (except for some kinds available in the United States) is too flimsy and leads to disappointing results.

Some suitable fabrics are:

Synthetic – coat or dress linings in Tricel, nylon, polyester, etc.

Cotton – curtain [drapery] lining, calico [unbleached muslin], cambric, cotton sateen.

Wool – As this is expensive it seems a pity to use it as a lining, but Viyella or Clydella, which are cotton/wool mixtures, provide warmth at relatively small cost.

THREADS

Although threads are virtually shrink-proof nowadays, it is a worthwhile precaution to match thread to fibres of fabric for quilting that is to be well washed. Sewing threads which are made for dressmaking are ideal, as they are readily available in a range of colours and can be used for machine or hand sewing. On the market are both cotton and synthetic sewing threads as well as pure silk sewing thread and buttonhole twist.

It is also possible to use embroidery thread, such as stranded cotton (1 to 3 strands), coton à broder or pearl cotton, sizes 12, 8 or 5. These threads are thicker than sewing threads (apart from 1 strand of stranded cotton) and give a bolder line of stitching.

FABRICS FOR SPECIFIC TECHNIQUES (TOP SURFACE)

The fabrics listed below are the ones most frequently used for specific techniques, but if you experiment you will find there are many other fabrics which can be used successfully.

English (wadded) quilting	
a) deep padding	jersey, jap [China] silk, lawn, felt, crepe, surah, hopsack, Viyella, suede, satin, gloving leather, cashmere, fine woollen dress fabrics, brushed nylon.
b) light or thin padding	dupion, poplin, dress cotton, polycotton, velvet, taffeta, wild [raw] silk, calico, denim, sateen.
Trapunto (stuffed) quilting	as for English quilting (a).
Italian – method 1	fine jersey, jap [China] silk, surah, crepe, Viyella, fine linen, lawn, fine suede, or gloving leather.
Italian – method 2	fine jersey, jap [China] silk, surah, crepe, Viyella, lawn.
Flat quilting	linen, satin, calico, taffeta, poplin, dress cottons, velvet, denim.
Quilting for patchwork	dress cottons, calico, and poplin.
Appliqué trapunto	poplin, calico, taffeta – aim for closely woven fabrics whose edges will not fray easily.
Shadow quilting	georgette, chiffon, organza.
See-through quilting	organdie, organza, georgette.
Machine-stitched Italian quilting	fine jersey, imitation suede, satin, fine linen.
Sprayed quilting	calico, jersey, satin.
Quilting patterned fabrics	dress cottons, chintz, gingham, jersey, Viyella, or printed woollens.

TECHNIQUES

Not everybody realizes how many different kinds of quilting there are. If you have enough time it is a good idea to work a small piece in each technique to find out if you like doing it and the effect it produces. These small pieces need not be wasted but could be made into pincushions, box tops or spectacle cases. The basic traditional techniques of quilting – English, trapunto and Italian – all have very practical applications on fashion clothing or in household items such as cushions [pillows], stool tops, tea cosies or even oven gloves, whereas shadow quilting and see-through quilting have more decorative possibilities in panels, hangings and room dividers, but could be applied to special items of dress.

You must first decide what you want to make and then choose the design and technique most suitable for its interpretation. The purpose of the item will also decide whether it will have to be washed or not, and this will dictate which fabrics will be the most appropriate. It is generally very unwise to attempt to iron quilting as this can flatten the padding, so for practical, washable articles aim to use drip-dry fabrics. Press all fabrics before you begin quilting.

The importance of thorough preparation cannot be over-stressed; it may seem tedious, but you will find it is essential if you wish to produce a piece of quilting with a really professional finish.

Thorough basting pays Nearly all forms of quilting are a sandwich of fabric, and, like any sandwich, if squeezed or pressured in one place will slip and slide in other directions. To prevent layers from slipping, thorough basting is essential. On large pieces work from the centre to the edge methodically, and on smaller pieces work successive parallel rows from one end to the other. Use as fine a thread and needle as possible and make the stitches firm, but do not pull tightly.

Always work from the centre outwards When stitching by hand or machine work from the centre outwards, to spread the layers evenly. On small pieces only, it is possible to work from one end to the other instead.

Allow for shrinkage Paddings take up room, so always allow extra fabric for 'shrinkage'; on large items or clothing, where thick padding is used in English quilting, the size can diminish considerably.

Work quilting on the fabric before cutting out Mark the pattern piece on the fabric with either tailors' chalk or tailor tacks and work the quilting within it. Then place the pattern piece on the fabric again; you may well find that the original shape needs adjustment because of shrinkage, before cutting out and making up the garment.

Complete the work in the following order:
1 Press fabrics (*not* wadding [padding]!).
2 Transfer design (except scratch marking on English quilting which is done between 3 & 4).
3 Layer fabrics, and baste thoroughly.
4 Stitch by hand or machine.
5 Remove basting (English quilting completed).
6 Pad trapunto or Italian quilting.

Hand and machine sewing

Today we have the choice of working by hand or with machine, both with equal success. There is little difference as regards final effect between hand back stitch and machine straight stitch; but running stitch has a less definite line, reverse chain stitch makes a very noticeable line, and zig-zag stitching on the machine can give several widths and variations of width in the stitch it makes.

HAND SEWING

To begin Use a small knot or darn the thread into the backing only, taking a single back stitch to secure it.
To finish Darn the thread into the stitchery on the wrong side and make a single back stitch for extra security.
Needles Use either sharps or crewel needles; size 8 for 50 sewing cotton, 7 for 40 sewing cotton and sizes 5 or 6 for buttonhole twist or pearl cotton.
Stitches of quilting are easily mastered but it is important to get tension right; pull the stitches firmly but not tightly. Aim to make your stitches as even as possible but not too small or the fabric is likely to pucker; about 2 mm ($\frac{1}{10}$ in) is the right length for most weights of fabric. Whether stitches can be scooped or will have to be stabbed vertically to and fro through the layers will depend very much on the thickness of fabric or padding. For thick fabrics and paddings stabbing will achieve the best results, but scooping is sometimes possible on the two layer techniques of trapunto and Italian quilting.

Back stitch will make a sharp incisive line. Make sure each stitch returns into the same hole as the previous stitch to form a sleek continuous line.

Running stitch makes a less definite line and also has the benefit of being reversible if carefully worked. Traditionally the stitching was worked very boldly on large quilts, to make an impact from a distance, rather than close up. It was also less time consuming than small stitching.

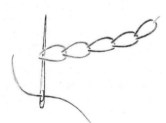

Reverse chain stitch was not used in traditional work, but makes a bold line where emphasis is needed. Be particularly careful not to pull this stitch tight.

Note: A form of running stitch well spaced in diagonal lines pulls English quilting into a diamond pattern suitable for padding the linings of boxes and tea-cosies.

In recent times it has been customary to work a whole piece in one stitch, but there is no reason why this should be so, as it adds variety to the work and the final effect if several stitches are combined on one piece.

Framing (for hand sewing)

Small pieces of work may be satisfactorily completed in the hand, but for the best results, in English quilting particularly, and for larger pieces, working in a frame of some sort is preferable. It leaves both hands free for quilting, and the work is not crushed. The *backing* only is framed very slackly, as tightly tensioned fabrics would prevent effective quilting by flattening the work. When the backing is mounted in the frame the process is continued as described previously. Basting is necessary, but the edges of the layers are not sewn to the backing or the frame.

The square embroidery frame (slate frame) is traditional and is the easiest to use. Once the backing has been sewn to the webbing it may be 'rolled in' round one roller, allowing only a comfortable working area to be revealed at a time.

To mount the backing
1 Ensure that the fabric is cut on the thread both ways.
2 Find the centre of one side by folding it in half and match this to the exact centre of the webbing on the roller.

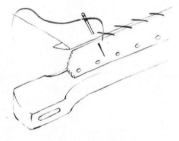

3 Turn in the edge of the fabric 6 mm ($\frac{1}{4}$ in) and oversew it to the webbing from the centre outwards in both directions. Sew the opposite side of the fabric to the other roller.

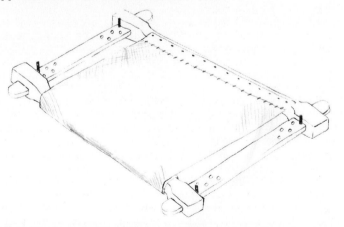

4 Roll in any excess backing on one roller, then place the slats (stretchers) in position and stretch lightly.

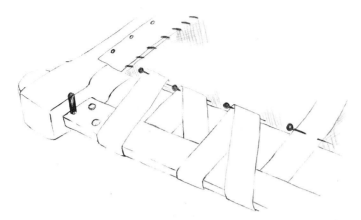

5 Strap out sides lightly with tape, alternately pinning it to the fabric and going over the slat before pinning to the fabric again.

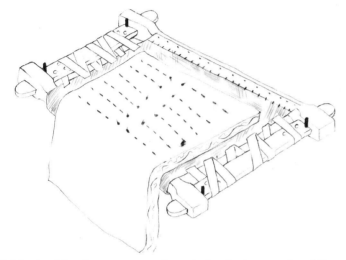

6 The backing is now mounted ready for the layers of wadding [padding] and top fabric to be added.

Baste these materials on top and continue preparation and sewing for the chosen technique, working outwards from this point. If the material is too long for the slats, roll the quilted fabric onto the other roller. This is the way the traditional quilts were sewn on large frames.

Frames

An embroidery frame (slate frame) is measured by the length of the webbing on the roller; the material to be framed may only be as wide as the webbing. It is best if the frame rests on a stand as this leaves both hands free for working. It should always be at a height convenient to the worker and placed in a good light.

For large quilts there are quilting frames which rest on their own trestles, but it is more usual for the frame to rest on the tops of two straight-backed chairs.

A simple adaption of a sturdy picture frame or artist's stretcher can be used as an alternative. The backing may be pinned on with thumb tacks or stapled to it or laced to it with string. Although this is only suitable for pieces which fit within the size of the frame available, as no rolling in is possible, a good result can nevertheless be achieved.

A circular frame (tambour frame or hoop) can be used if the whole design fits within it. However, wadding [padding] pressed between the two rings of a frame would be badly squashed, and the drawback of this type of frame is that it can crush or mark fabric permanently – so any kind of quilting must be slackly stretched in this frame, too.

MACHINE SEWING

Always refer to your machine handbook for instructions on quilting, as each machine has different capabilities and the fittings supplied by different manufacturers vary greatly.

Preparation of work   It can be most annoying to machine through rows of basting that constantly catch under the foot, so it is often preferable to pin all the layers together using the finest pins available, and remove them as the work progresses. Pin at about 5 cm (2 in) intervals all over, working from centre to edge as for basting.

Needles   A size 14 (90) machine needle is best for 40 or 50 sewing cotton. Make sure the tip is not worn and blunted or it will not penetrate the layers well, and will therefore miss stitches.

If all your layers are synthetic a ball point needle of the same size is worth considering.

For leather or suede always use a leather needle.

Starting and finishing   Leave long ends, draw them through to the wrong side, tie them and cut ends as close to the work as possible.

Straight stitch   Set the stitch length to about 2 mm ($\frac{1}{10}$ in). Check to see if your machine has a quilting foot, which may also have an attachment for spacing rows.

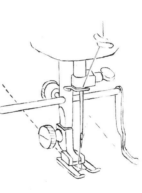

Always work rows in the same direction to prevent the fabric pulling in opposite directions, causing puckering. Simple straight lines and check or diamond patterns may be worked directly onto the fabric using the spacing attachment to maintain equal distances between the lines, or by gauging width by eye. This avoids unnecessary marking of lines on the fabric.

Patterns or designs with gentle curves can also be worked by machine, but unless you have a lot of patience, avoid small intricate patterns which require constant stopping and starting.

Machine quilting can also be worked from the wrong side, allowing the design to be traced on to the backing.

Zig-zag stitch   This stitch can be used in the same way as straight stitch, but the stitch length may be varied from almost nil, giving a satin stitch line, to 2 mm ($\frac{1}{10}$ in) which will give a very open zig-zag. With experience the stitch width can also be varied while stitching, giving a line of varied thickness with a rippling effect.

Use of pre-set pattern   Many machines nowadays have pre-set patterns and these may be combined with quilting to great effect; simple bands of stitchery are likely to be more effective than a complex pattern with a textured line.

'Free' machine quilting   Not all machines are suitable for this technique but check by experimenting with your machine, as it means that stitching can be worked in any direction and within small areas, making it ideal for the initial stitching in trapunto and Italian quilting.

Prepare the machine for machine embroidery, following the instruction booklet for your machine; place the work in a circular frame (hoop), stretching the fabrics firmly, and machine around the outline of the design. Continue, following the instructions for trapunto and Italian quilting.

Some machines also have a darning or embroidery foot which can be used to work very intricate designs. It will also enable you to embroider English quilting freely without using a frame, and thus avoid squashing the wadding [padding] and marking the fabric permanently.

ENGLISH OR WADDED QUILTING

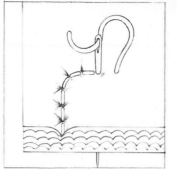

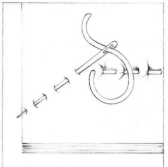

Before you begin quilting make sure all the recommended preparation has been done; thorough basting is essential. If you are using paper-backed wadding [padding] open it out and make sure the fluffy side is always uppermost. Begin by making a small knot in the thread; then bring the needle through from the wrong side and give the thread a gentle tug, which will pull the knot through the backing to lodge in the padding. Working from the right side, start quilting from the centre outwards to ensure even spreading of the layers. When working through thick layering, stab the needle up and down, but for thinner layers – for example, a single layer of domette – you may be able to take several running stitches on the needle at once. Stitches should be about 2 mm ($\frac{1}{10}$ in) long, whether back or running, and pulled down firmly but not tightly. If your work puckers, you may be either taking too short a stitch or pulling too tightly.

TRAPUNTO OR STUFFED QUILTING

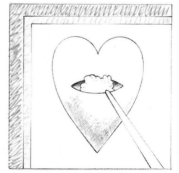

For this technique, two layers of fabric are joined together along the design lines by stitching and then selected areas are padded. To do this, baste as previously directed, then back stitch, running stitch or machine stitch along the design outline. Turn it to the wrong side and make a small slit in the centre of the shape, through the backing only, and on the grain if possible. Tease out the padding by pulling it apart and push in a small piece at a time with a knitting needle, until the shape stands out in relief. If your padding feels lumpy you are either trying to put in too much at a time, or not pushing each piece in far enough. With experience you will find it is possible to pad very softly or, if the top layer is very stretchy, to achieve a very raised effect by pushing in a lot of padding. Lastly sew up the slit as shown in the diagram.

ITALIAN OR CORDED QUILTING

This can be either a two layer or one layer technique, but for both the design must be planned in parallel lines about 4 mm ($\frac{1}{6}$ in) apart.

Method 1 Using two layers of fabric, first transfer the design onto the backing. Then, using running stitch or machine stitching, sew the two layers together from the wrong side. Thread a bold tapestry needle with quilting wool or similar, insert it through the backing only and manipulate it between the lines of stitching. To get around corners, bring the needle out through the backing and then re-insert it in the same hole leaving a small loop of wool to allow for stretching. If the backing is firm use a stiletto for making the initial holes for threading. Leave short ends of quilting wool to allow for shrinkage.

Method 2 Using one layer of stretchy fabric, first transfer the design onto the wrong side. Lay either quilting wool, cord or similar between the marked lines and sew down firmly with a closed herringbone stitch. This must be worked with care to produce a neat line of stitching on the right side.

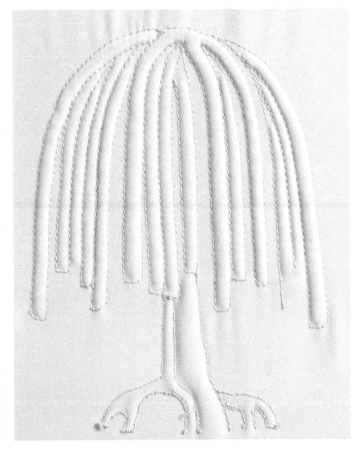

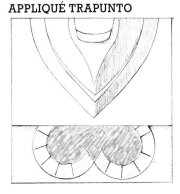

APPLIQUÉ TRAPUNTO

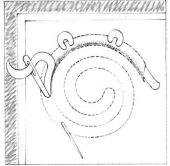

This technique combines appliqué and trapunto and is a means of incorporating colour in your quilting. First apply pieces of closely woven fabric such as poplin to a firm backing. This can be done in one of two ways: either turn under the edge of the shape and hem it firmly to the backing with small stitches, or turn under the edge and machine with a straight stitch or zig-zag to sew it firmly in place. Then turn the backing to the wrong side; make a small slit in the centre of the shape and push in padding. Follow the trapunto technique to finish.

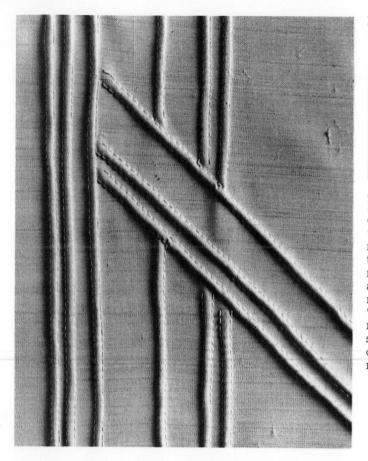

MACHINE-STITCHED ITALIAN QUILTING

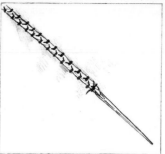

An effect of Italian quilting can be produced on a single layer of fabric by using the broadest twin needle in a sewing machine. You may have to refer to your instruction book or manufacturer to find out if this accessory is made for your machine.

Transfer the design onto the right side of the fabric; use a single layer of fabric, such as crepe or fine jersey, and twin needle the design. On some machines cord can be inserted while machining, but otherwise quilting wool or similar yarns can be inserted under the stitching on the wrong side to form a crisp raised line. If matching thread is used in one needle and a darker shade in the other, a shadow can be suggested to emphasize the raised effect. This technique is very well integrated with the fabric so it is ideal for dress or home furnishings.

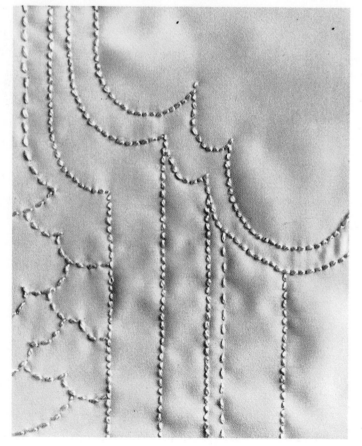

FLAT QUILTING

Two layers of fabric stitched together will act as a slight padding for each other and the surface becomes both rich and textured. The design is not limited by the technique but a series of small shapes is generally more effective than large ones. Sew the two layers together along the design lines working from the centre outwards, either with back stitch, chain stitch, running stitch or machine stitching. Because there is no raised padding the stitched line is important and can be emphasized by using a thick thread such as pearl cotton No. 8 or 5, which will give a bead-like effect.

This technique is particularly suitable for decorative effects on clothing as it adds texture without bulk.

WORKING WITH PATTERNED FABRICS

So far the techniques described have been worked on plain fabrics on which a design has been drawn or traced, but there is no reason why fabrics having a printed pattern should not be enhanced with quilting. There are two methods which are most commonly used for quilting patterned fabrics:

a) Use a fabric with a spaced sprig motif and superimpose a pattern of diamonds, grids, or curved lines between the motifs, working either in English or Italian quilting.

b) Use a fabric with a bold overall design and either English quilt around each shape, or trapunto quilt chosen areas, for example a bold flower, and perhaps flat quilt the rest.

Select printed fabrics with care; a very bold pattern can entirely hide any quilting worked on it.

Another exciting approach is to quilt striped fabrics using the Italian method. The lines of quilting may follow the existing pattern of stripes or cut across them to add a new dimension to the design. Repeating patterns such as spots can also be altered dramatically by quilting different shapes onto them.

QUILTED PATCHWORK

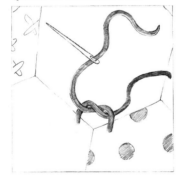

It is possible to English quilt patchwork when the patchwork is completed, but there is a special technique for tying down the layers in a padded patchwork quilt. This is done by means of individual knots, usually only at the points of selected template shapes. Each knot is worked separately. Thread a needle with strong thread, and starting on the right side, take it down through the layers out through the backing and then back up to the right side leaving a small 'stitch' on the backing. Tie a simple knot on the right side, and finally take both ends through to the wrong side and tie a double knot, cutting the ends as close as is practicable. This technique can also be applied when a 'spot' rather than a line effect is required in English quilting.

SHADOW QUILTING

This can be achieved by using a transparent fabric such as chiffon or georgette for the top layer, a firm backing, and then following the Italian or trapunto technique. Always use strong, clear colours for paddings as they become very muted.

Follow Method 1 Italian quilting, but use coloured yarns to thread between the fabric channels.

Follow the trapunto technique, but pad with scraps of coloured fabric or dyed wadding or 'scrambled' yarns. These techniques are largely experimental and decorative, but by combining materials of the same substance, for example, all synthetic, it is possible to apply them to articles of utilitarian use in the home and on dress.

SEE-THROUGH QUILTING

See-through quilting is an extension of the previous technique. By using two layers of a transparent fabric, such as organdie, you can create a see-through reversible effect. This could be useful for a room divider or a hanging against a window, or a lampshade. For this method the 'decoration' of coloured fabrics – or perhaps tinsel or sequins – is sandwiched in between two transparent layers and then held in place by outlining with running stitch or machine stitching. Particular care must be taken with finishing ends so that they are not visible – darning in is probably the best solution. This form of quilting is often decorated by embroidery stitches.

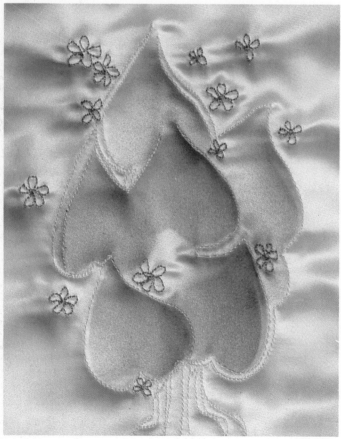

SPRAYED QUILTING

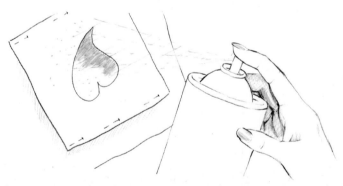

Spray painting can be used in two ways to enhance quilting: by spraying the fabric with coloured areas, you can introduce extra colour to quilting; by spraying quilting already completed from a very low angle, you can enhance the shadows and make the quilting look even more three dimensional. For an entirely decorative effect car spray paints can be used; these do not stiffen the fabric, as many people imagine. Otherwise, fabric paints and dyes may be used in a spray gun, but you may find that these are not permanent when subjected to frequent washing. Spraying is particularly suited to experimental decorative work and to theatrical costumes. Very attractive effects can be achieved by merging the colour sprays. If a clear design is required, cut paper masks to cover the areas not to be coloured and pin in position, near the edge, to give a sharp line. Pin a little further back if a softer, less distinct outline is preferred.

MAKING UP QUILTING

Because of the layering, which is part of nearly all quilting, making up can present problems if the material is very bulky. It is advisable not to trim any layer away until all have been secured within the edge or seam.

Binding is a neat way to finish an edge on a quilted garment, a waistcoat [vest] for example, or a table mat. Either use a crossway [bias] strip of fabric about 2.5 cm (1 in) wide, or bought binding, and baste, then machine it 6 mm (¼ in) from the edge on the right side. If you are using wadding [padding], ensure that all the layers are sewn together before trimming the wadding [padding] as near to the stitching as possible, and trim any surplus width off in the other layers. Turn the binding over and hem on the wrong side. Binding strips can be cut on the sraight grain of the fabric for large quilts and other articles with straight sides. Binding can also be used on cushions [pillows], tea cosies and even totebags as an alternative to piping.

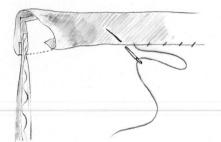

Facing is an alternative way to create a neat edge. Cut a piece of fabric on the straight to match the shape of the edge to be faced, about 5 cm (2 in) wide. Baste it to the right side of the quilting, edges matching, and machine about 6 mm (¼ in) from the edge. Trim away any wadding [padding] and the backing very close to the stitching. Turn the facing over entirely to the wrong side, rolling it under gently so that the seam line lies just to the inside. Press, and hem to the backing. Facing is suitable for necklines and hems on clothing.

Piping is a crossway [bias] strip folded in half lengthwise to cover a piping cord, and is sewn between the facing and the quilting. It is particularly useful for finishing cushions [pillows].

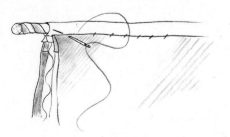

Quilt edges are traditionally turned in, as is the backing, and the two edges are running stitched together.

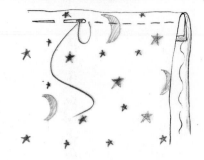

Seaming There are two methods for seaming quilted materials together:

a) Baste seams together on the wrong side about 1 cm (½ in) from the edge, making sure all the layers are smooth and in no way pleated or wrinkled. Machine on the seam line; trim away any wadding [padding] as close to the stitching as possible and trim the backing almost to the stitching. Open the seam flat, and neaten the edges by oversewing or zig-zagging.

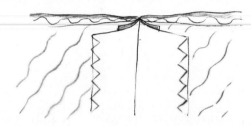

b) Seam as before, but after trimming the wadding [padding] close to the stitching, trim the other layers to 6 mm (¼ in) and bind to neaten.

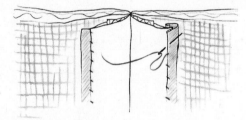

TRANSFERRING DESIGNS

When transferring a design onto fabric there are some things which should never be used: a ball point pen is very messy and will stain the thread and fabric; a felt tip pen tends to spread to a wide line and also stains the fabric; a heavy pencil line will dirty the thread and fabric; carbon paper leaves a permanent line and can colour the thread and fabric.

Scratch marking

This is the traditional tracing technique used for English quilting. After the quilting is fully prepared on the frame, the template is laid in position and a needle pressed firmly all around its outline. This leaves a clear crease line on the top fabric for just long enough to work the quilting. This technique relies on natural fibres such as cotton or linen, as on those modern fabrics which are all synthetic, or have a high synthetic content, the fibres immediately spring back in position and the scratch marking leaves no line. So this method can only be used successfully on silk, cotton, or linen for template-based designs.

Dressmakers' tracing paper

Dressmakers' tracing paper is sold in several colours, including white, yellow, red and blue, and is a kind of carbon paper. Choose a colour to contrast with your fabric. Place the fabric on a flat surface, put the tracing paper face side down on it and the outline design on top; pin or weight all the layers together but make sure there is no undue pressure on the work to make unwanted smudges. Using a sharply pointed pencil, mark around the outline of the design. When you think it is completed, lift one corner to make sure and then remove design and tracing paper. Make sure dressmakers' tracing paper will work on your fabric by first having a trial run; once marked the line is permanent.

Tracing

Draw the design on white paper with a simple bold outline in black felt tip pen. Place the design on a white flat surface, put the material on top, then pin or weight them together in position. Trace the outline through with a dressmakers' pencil, a very sharp HB [medium] pencil or a fine brush and watercolour paint. It is surprising how many fabrics which look opaque are not, and this method can often be used on cottons, crepes, satins, calico and others. Dressmakers' pencil does not leave a permanent mark so this is not suitable for large complex designs which may take some time to work, but HB [medium] pencil and a painted line will last.

Tracing and basting

Trace the design onto a piece of tissue paper, in simple outline; pin the paper to the fabric at the edges and sew in a bold running stitch or small basting stitch, through paper and fabric – following the outline of the design and taking care to secure the ends thoroughly. Remove the pins and tear off the tissue paper leaving the design in basted outline. The basting is removed as the quilting is completed.

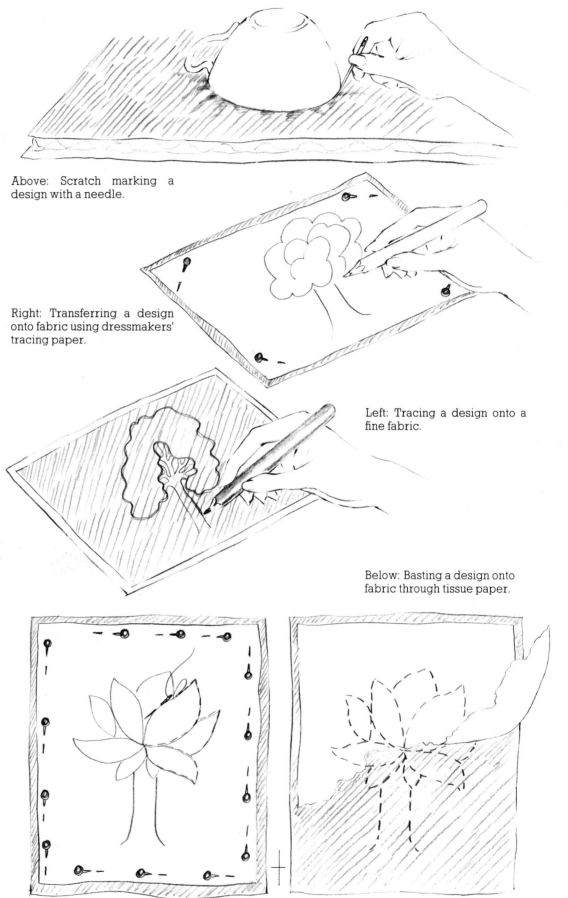

Above: Scratch marking a design with a needle.

Right: Transferring a design onto fabric using dressmakers' tracing paper.

Left: Tracing a design onto a fine fabric.

Below: Basting a design onto fabric through tissue paper.

25

BEGINNERS' PATTERNS

The quilted workbag and workbasket are perfect beginners' patterns. Not only are they very simple to make, but, when finished, they will provide homes for all the sewing materials you will require for the more advanced projects. The little purse can also be used for storing items such as fine scissors and tape measures or needles and pins.

The quilting designs for the cushion [pillow] are worked on a frame. You will find complete instructions for mounting work in a frame on pages 16 to 17, and further details about English (wadded) quilting on page 18.

Quilted workbag

Finished size: 25 × 30 cm (10 × 12 in)

MATERIALS

46 × 60 cm (18 × 24 in) piece of printed fabric

46 × 60 cm (18 × 24 in) piece of synthetic wadding [padding]

46 × 60 cm (18 × 24 in) piece of lining fabric

Pair of wooden bag handles, approximately 30 cm (12 in) long

Matching sewing thread

TO MAKE THE WORKBAG

Lay printed fabric right side up on top of wadding [padding] and pin. Baste fabric and wadding [padding] together from top to bottom and from side to side, making lines approximately 3 cm (1¼ in) apart. Quilt the materials together, following the basted lines with lines of straight machine stitching.

To make up

Place quilted fabric right side up; lay lining fabric face down on top. Stitch all around, 1 cm (⅜ in) from raw edge, leaving a 10 cm (4 in) gap on one side for turning bag right side out.

Turn bag right side out and lightly press. Slip stitch opening together so that all raw edges are enclosed.

To attach handles

Pull one short end of bag through the gap on one handle. Allow a turning [seam] of no more than 4 cm (1½ in) and machine stitch through all layers, keeping as close to the handle as possible (**fig. 1**). You will have to stitch bit by bit, pushing each completed section of stitching along, as the bag is wider than the opening on the handle. Repeat for the second handle.

Fold bag in half, right sides together, with the handles at the top. Place a pin through all six layers of material on each side just below handles. Measure down 7.5 cm (3 in) from bottom of handles and place another pin.

Machine stitch sides from lower pin to bottom of bag. For extra strength, go over the stitching at the top a few times. Fasten off and turn bag right side out.

Quilted workbasket

Materials given are for a round basket 23 cm (9 in) in diameter and 7.5 cm (3 in) deep.

MATERIALS

Scraps of fabric for patchwork lid

25 cm (10 in) square of fabric for backing

40 cm (16 in) square of fabric for lining basket

40 × 81 cm (16 × 32 in) length of synthetic wadding [padding]

77 cm (30 in) bias binding

Matching sewing thread

Stiff paper

Pencil

Basket

TO MAKE THE BASKET LID

Turn basket upside down on paper and draw around rim. Cut out the circle, fold it in half and cut along the fold. Repeat the folding and cutting with one half, then with one quarter to obtain a wedge-shaped pattern for one-eighth of a circle. Use this to cut eight pieces of fabric, adding 1 cm (⅜ in) all around for seams.

Join patchwork together into two semi-circles of four pieces each.

Make a small loop of bias binding and sew securely to lower edge of one semi-circle. Sew the two semi-circles together taking care to match seams at the centre. Press seams flat.

Cut two circles of wadding [padding] and one piece of

backing fabric to same size as the patchwork. Place backing fabric face down, lay the circles of wadding [padding] and the patchwork on top. Pin, then baste along all eight seams. Machine stitch along all seams working from the centre outwards.

Trim raw edge, then bind all around circle edge.

To line the basket

Cut lining fabric to a 40 cm (16 in) diameter circle. Cut wadding [padding] 1 cm (⅜ in) smaller all around.

Place fabric right side down; lay wadding [padding] on top. Fold raw edge of fabric over wadding [padding] and make small gathering stitches all around.

Place lining inside basket and draw up gathering thread to fit. Fasten securely.

Stitch lining to basket, taking stitches around the woven strands of the basket.

To measure a basket of any size

You can easily determine the materials required to fit a basket of any size.

Turn basket upside down and draw round rim. This gives circular pattern for lid.

To obtain measurements for lining, add twice depth measurement to diameter, or measure down one side, across the base and up the other side. Add extra for seam allowance.

Quilted cushion [pillow]

Cushion can be made to any size required

MATERIALS

Synthetic silk (ie: dress lining) sufficient to cut two pieces of fabric the same size as required for the cushion, plus 22 cm (9 in)

Synthetic wadding [padding], same size as cushion

Lightweight backing fabric, slightly larger than cushion

Matching synthetic sewing thread

Matching synthetic thread, slightly heavier, for quilting

Tracing paper

Dressmakers' paper

Slate frame

Cushion pad [pillow form]

TO MAKE THE CUSHION

Cut one square of fabric same size as cushion pad [pillow form], and one square for quilting 3 cm (1¼ in) larger all round. The finished cover should be slightly smaller than the pad for a firm fit, but extra fabric is required for mounting in the frame.

Cut two strips 4 cm (1½ in) wide for the frill from the whole width of fabric, and one strip 2 cm (¾ in) wide and the length of one side of the cushion for the facing.

Enlarge one of the designs (**fig. 1**), leaving 5 cm (2 in) all round. Position tracing on larger square of fabric, near one edge, allowing for the seam. Secure tracing with pins along three sides. Slide a piece of dressmakers' carbon under the tracing and trace design onto the fabric.

Repeat along the other three sides of the cushion cover.

Quilting the design

Mount backing in the slate frame. Baste fabric, wadding [padding] and backing together, working from centre outwards.

Work the quilting in small, regular back stitches, working from the centre outwards. As a section of the quilting is completed, remove the basting threads.

Preparing the frill

Join the two strips of fabric into a ring and fold in half lengthwise. Press.

Make small pleats along the entire length so that the frill fits the circumference of the cushion cover, allowing for easing at the corners.

Sew the pleats by hand or machine 3 mm (⅛ in) from raw edge. Press.

To finish

Trim quilted fabric to same size as back piece of cushion cover. Sew facing 1 cm (⅜ in) from edge along one side of back piece. Machine stitch or hand hem raw edge of facing.

Baste frill to right side of quilted fabric, with edge facing inwards and easing corners. Machine stitch along one edge.

Place back of cover right side down on top piece with faced side aligned with attached side of frill. Machine stitch around remaining three sides, 1 cm (⅜ in) from edge. Overcast raw edges.

Turn right side out, ensuring that corners are well pushed out. Insert cushion pad [pillow form] and slip stitch opening.

Quilted purse

Finished size: 12 × 15 cm (5 × 6 in)

MATERIALS

15 × 30 cm (6 × 12 in) length of printed fabric

15 × 30 cm (6 × 12 in) length of wadding [padding]

15 × 30 cm (6 × 12 in) length of lining fabric

65 cm (26 in) length of silk binding or bias binding

Matching sewing thread

One hammer-in snap fastener

TO MAKE THE PURSE

Lay fabric, wadding [padding] and lining together. Pin through all three layers and then baste diagonally across the fabrics, working from the centre outwards.

Quilt the materials together following the basting lines with straight machine stitching.

To finish

Lay quilted fabric flat. Trim away untidy edges and cut one end into a curve (**fig. 1**).

Bind short straight edge.

Lay purse flat with lining uppermost and fold straight edge up 10 cm (4 in). Pin at both corners and machine stitch down both sides (**fig. 2**).

Bind all raw edges, tucking binding in at two bottom corners for a neat finish.

Attach snap fastener to the flap of the purse following the manufacturers' instructions.

DESIGN

HOW TO DESIGN YOUR WORK

Many people feel daunted by the prospect of trying to design their own work. They often feel they do not have the right experience or artistic ability. But by starting with simple patterns, using templates, you will acquire confidence, and then it is possible to take the next step, which is to attempt more ambitious shapes. This section gives instructions for the sort of techniques that can be employed. However there are one or two points to bear in mind. The first seems obvious: *decide the size of what you are going to make.* If you are taking the trouble to design your own work and spend hours sewing it, then it is worth making sure it fits from the start. Measure precisely the size of what you are going to make, be it pochette bag, panel or cushion [pillow], and draw the outline on paper or make a paper pattern.

Secondly, decide what technique you are going to use. Rounded flowing lines look good in English quilting, Italian quilting needs double lines, trapunto needs sufficiently large areas to pad and these must be provided at the design stage. Thirdly, designs cannot be drawn 'off the top of your head' if you have not fed any ideas into it! Even very talented artists and designers have to work from actual objects, at least to start with, so make sure you have a clear photograph, a drawing or even an object to refer to before you begin designing. It is a good idea to keep a scrap book containing magazine cuttings, postcards and perhaps your own sketches – a collection of visual ideas that appeal to you.

Don't inhibit yourself by buying an expensive piece of beautiful white paper to draw your first design on. Begin by working on handy pieces of scrap paper, because you will need to make several attempts before reaching a final design. Keep a supply of tracing paper (greaseproof is a good alternative) so that you can trace off the bits you like and discard what you do not like rather than doing a lot of erasing.

Where do ideas for designs come from? There is a design hidden in almost everything that you see, including buildings, cars, trees and flowers, as well as other crafts like wrought iron, or jewellery. The important thing is to choose what appeals to you personally.

The delicate lines on a butterfly's wings provide the quilter with pleasing shapes on which to base a design.

Developing a series of designs from one source

Draw or trace the outline of a butterfly; this drawing could be adapted to the back of a jacket, a tea cosy or a transparent hanging. Develop one wing by doodling your own patterns into it, echoing the lines already there: this could also be used for dress decoration or shadow quilting on a 'free' panel. Choose a section of this design by moving a round or square frame over it until a suitable 'abstraction' is found. Trace off this area. This design can be enlarged for a cushion or a panel or used actual size in a clear paper weight. Or repeat the design to form a border pattern which could become the frame for a mirror, a belt or decoration on a cuff.

Designing from another craft – wrought iron

Begin by drawing a gate, for example, or tracing from a picture. Decide whether you can use the whole of it, or only a section; what you are aiming at is a simple linear design that you can quilt, so ignore small detail. Perhaps a section is all that is necessary to make a border, a motif or an overall design.

Below: A tracing of the whole wrought iron design.

Above: A simplified version of the original design. The outlined shapes have been selected for making up new designs.

Attractive designs can be developed by linking and repeating one simple motif. The arrangement of shapes into 'mirror' patterns is also very effective.

EASY PATTERNS

Many patterns on traditional quilts are formed by template shapes reproduced again and again in order to construct repeating patterns. The template must be made in a firm substance, such as card [cardboard], lace-making card or parchment, whose edges will not bend or wear too quickly. Cut the shape from card with a very sharp knife and make a mark, or marks, on the edges to ensure it will meet its neighbour in the same place each time.

These patterns may be transferred onto English quilting by scratch marking or in tailors' chalk, if they are to be worked quickly. Otherwise draw out the whole design on paper and transfer it to the fabric using any of the other methods described on page 25. In Welsh quilts the templates are 12.5 cm (5 in) long to make bold patterns in keeping with the scale of the quilt.

A variety of repeating border patterns can be developed from the simple leaf template.

Above: Circle template marked with notches to link pattern.

Above: Freehand spiral pattern. Below: 'Wineglass' pattern formed by intersecting circles.

The heart motif is associated with wedding and engagement quilts. It can be used effectively as a border pattern or motif.

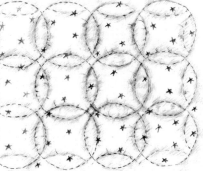

Many unusual repeating border and filler patterns are based upon simple half and quarter circles.

Large template outlines are traced onto the fabric and additional decoration worked freehand to create a richer design.

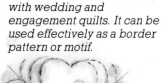

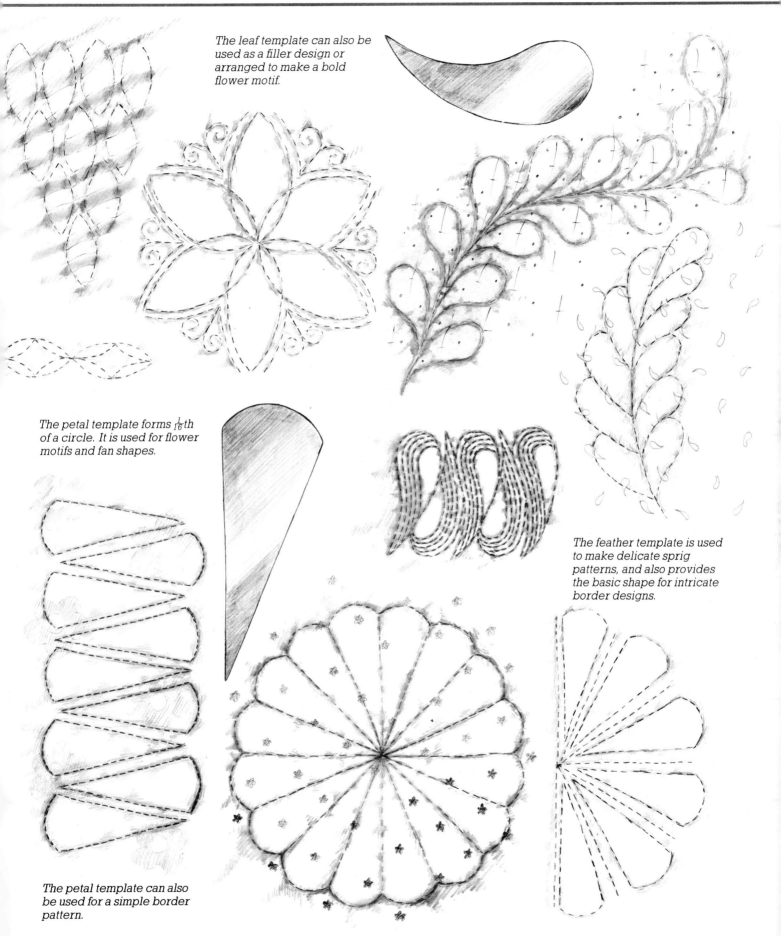

The leaf template can also be used as a filler design or arranged to make a bold flower motif.

The petal template forms $\frac{1}{16}$th of a circle. It is used for flower motifs and fan shapes.

The feather template is used to make delicate sprig patterns, and also provides the basic shape for intricate border designs.

The petal template can also be used for a simple border pattern.

PROJECTS

The following pages contain a variety of beautifully designed projects for you to make. The ideas range from quilted garments for children and adults to cushions [pillows], bedcovers and wall hangings.

Every project is illustrated in colour with clear step-by-step instructions and diagrams.

The patterns include simple beginners' projects and more advanced designs for the experienced needlewoman.

Throughout the patterns measurements are given in metric followed by the imperial equivalent in parentheses.

QUILTED TEA COSY

SATIN CUSHIONS [PILLOWS]

The refreshingly pretty satin cushions [pillows] and tea cosy photographed on this page are excellent examples of the ways in which modern quilting can be used to add a touch of luxury to your home.

Circular patterned satin cushion [pillow]

Finished size: 40 cm (16 in) square

MATERIALS

1 m (39 in) cream satin, 90 cm (36 in) wide

50 cm (20 in) square piece of synthetic wadding [padding]

1 m (39 in) calico [unbleached cotton] for lining

Approximately 4 m (4¼ yd) piping, covered with cotton floral print

1 packet each, pink and green clear glass beads

Synthetic machine thread in various pastel colours

Tracing paper, 40 cm (16 in) square

Pencil

Pair of compasses [compass]

Cushion pad [pillow form], 40 cm (16 in) square

TO MAKE THE CUSHION

Cut out satin, wadding [padding] and lining all approximately 46 cm (18 in) square.

Enlarge central flower design (**fig. 1**), so that the central area measures 9 cm (3½ in). Trace it onto centre of tracing paper. Set the compasses to a radius of 4.5 cm (1¾ in) and draw a circle over the flower design on tracing. Position other circles on the tracing paper, following

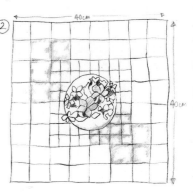

the arrangement in **fig. 2**.
Baste tracing paper to the satin, wadding [padding] and lining, working from the centre outwards.

Working the pattern

Hand embroider the central flower design in stem stitch, through the tracing paper and fabrics, using machine sewing thread.

Machine stitch around the circular pattern in straight stitch, using the darning foot. Remove all tracing paper.

With free machine stitching, decorate circle centres (**fig. 3**) using mainly cream machine sewing thread with occasional pink centres for variety.

Sew on a glass bead at each point where circles meet.

Pin and baste piping in place around edges of cushion on the right side (**fig. 4** opposite page).

To finish

Cut the backing from the remaining satin, leaving a generous seam allowance.

With right sides facing, sew the cushion front to the backing, leaving one side open. Overcast raw edges. Turn cushion cover right side out and insert pad [pillow form]. Slip stitch opening.

Square patterned satin cushion [pillow]

Finished size: 40 cm (16 in) square

MATERIALS

1 m (39 in) cream satin, 90 cm (36 in) wide

50 cm (20 in) square piece of synthetic wadding [padding]

1 m (39 in) calico [unbleached cotton] for lining

Approximately 4 m (4¼ yd) piping, covered with cotton floral print

1 packet each, pink and green clear glass beads

Synthetic machine thread in various pastel colours

Tracing paper

Pencil

Pair of compasses [compass]

Cushion pad [pillow form], 40 cm (16 in) square

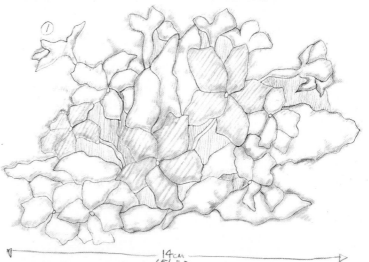

TO MAKE THE CUSHION

Cut out satin, wadding [padding] and lining all approximately 46 cm (18 in) square.

Enlarge flower design (**fig. 1**), so that it measures approximately 14 cm (5½ in) in width, and trace it on to centre of tracing paper. Set the compasses to a radius of 5.5 cm (2 in) and draw a circle over the flower design on the tracing. Divide remaining area of the paper into squares measuring

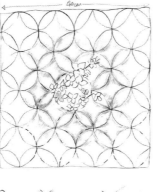

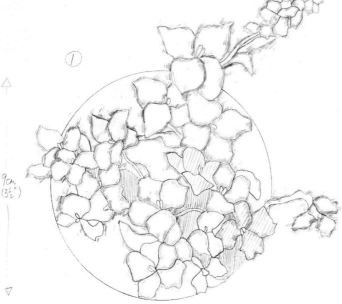

2.5 cm (1 in) and 5 cm (2 in) as shown (**fig. 2**).
Baste tracing paper to the satin, wadding [padding] and lining, working from the centre.

Working the pattern

Hand embroider the central flower design in stem stitch, through the paper and fabrics, using machine sewing thread. Machine stitch the pattern of squares from the centre outwards, using the zig-zag foot and straight stitch. Remove all tracing paper. Set sewing machine to pattern stitches of

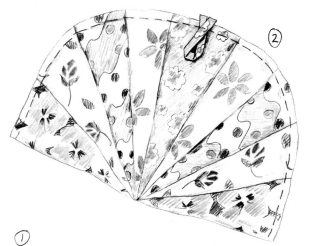

your choice; work each pattern in stripes of different colours in each alternate square (**fig. 3**). Sew on a glass bead at each

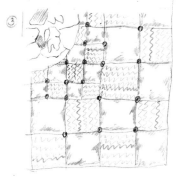

point where squares meet.
Pin and baste piping in place along outer stitch line (**fig. 4**).

To finish

Cut the backing from the remaining satin, leaving a generous seam allowance. With right sides facing, sew the cushion front to the backing, leaving one side open. Overcast raw edges. Turn cushion cover the right way and insert pad [pillow form]. Slip stitch opening.

Quilted tea cosy

Finished size: 20 × 38 cm (8 × 15 in)

MATERIALS

Scraps of cotton print fabric for front and back

40 × 50 cm (16 × 20 in) piece of synthetic wadding [padding]

40 × 50 cm (16 × 20 in) piece of lining fabric

Extra scraps of wadding [padding] for quilting the patchwork

1 m (39 in) bias strip 4 cm (1½ in) wide (regular bias binding is too narrow)

Matching sewing thread

Paper

Pencil

TO MAKE THE COSY

Make up a paper pattern following the diagram (**fig. 1**). Cut the pattern into nine segments, number each one and use these as templates to cut out the 18 pieces of fabric that make up the back and front of the cosy. Add 1 cm (⅜ in) all around for seams when cutting out the fabric.
Stitch the segments together to make up a back and a front. Press seams open lightly.

Cut two pieces of lining fabric and two pieces of wadding [padding] the same size as the patchwork front and back.
Place front piece face up, lay lining face down on top and place wadding [padding] on top of the lining.
Stitch all three layers together along the bottom edge only.
Turn right side out. Repeat for back.

Quilting the fabric

Pin each seam of the patchwork through all three layers. Baste and then machine stitch through each seam, working from the centre outwards and from the bottom to the top each time.
Cut extra strips of wadding [padding] to fit and push down into each section between the top fabric and the wadding [padding]. Use a knitting needle to push the wadding [padding] down. Repeat for back.

To finish

Place back and front together, right sides out, and matching each seam to its corresponding seam on the other side.
Pin through all six layers.
Machine stitch the two halves together and trim raw edges. Make a small loop from a scrap of binding and sew to centre panel (**fig. 2**). Bind raw edge.

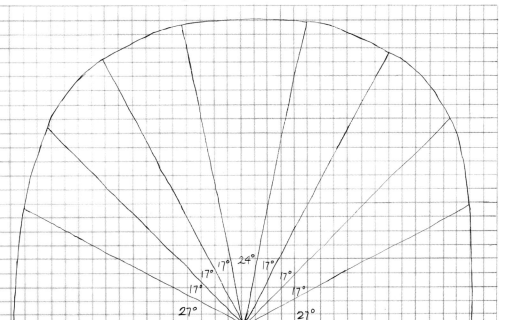

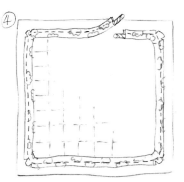

BIRTHDAY CUSHION [PILLOW]
APPLIQUÉ PICTURE

The picture and birthday cushion [pillow] are examples of modern appliqué. Traditionally, the edges of appliquéd motifs are finished with a decorative embroidery stitch around the raw edges.

A couching technique is used on the cushion [pillow] for the 'Happy Birthday' and scalloped pattern on the side of the cake. In couching, ribbons, cords or threads are laid on the surface of the fabric and held in place with a finer thread – the couching thread – with small stitches. This method is often used to conceal, and decorate, the raw edge of a motif. For the design on the birthday cake, draw the six strands of thread and the couching thread through to the surface. Using one hand to guide the laid threads, secure them in position by making tiny overcasting stitches with the couching thread at regular intervals.

Birthday cushion [pillow]

Finished size: 40 cm (16 in) square

MATERIALS

1 m (39 in) pale lilac shiny satin, 90 cm (36 in) wide

20 cm (8 in) medium lilac shiny satin, 90 cm (36 in) wide

25 cm (10 in) white shiny satin, 90 cm (36 in) wide

28 cm (11 in) square white faille

50 cm (20 in) synthetic wadding [padding], 90 cm (36 in) wide

100 cm (40 in) calico [unbleached cotton], 90 cm (36 in) wide

10 cm (4 in) square white leather or felt

50 cm (20 in) pale blue velvet ribbon, 2.5 cm (1 in) wide

180 cm (70 in) white cord

36 cm (14 in) lilac zipper

Stranded embroidery thread in white and pink

Sewing thread in white and lilac

Dressmakers' graph paper

Cushion pad [pillow form] 40 cm (16 in) square

TO MAKE THE CUSHION

Cutting out the fabric

Enlarge the design in **fig. 1** and make paper patterns for the plate and cake shapes.

From the pale lilac satin cut one 44 cm (17½ in) square and two pieces 25 × 44 cm (10 × 17½ in). Also cut the plate piece, using the paper pattern and adding 1 cm (⅜ in) seam allowance.

Cut the top of the cake from the shiny white satin and the side from the faille, adding on the seam allowance. Cut the faille so that the ribs run vertically on the cakes.

Cut a 44 cm (17½ in) square of wadding [padding].

From the calico [unbleached cotton] cut one backing piece 44 cm (17½ in) square and seven small pieces each 25 cm (10 in) square.

Working the design

Begin with the plate. Turn in the seam allowance round the outside curve and baste. Pin the plate to the background square of satin so that the weave is at right angles to the weave of the background. This will create the effect of a subtle difference in shades.

Slip stitch in place, then baste inside curve down onto background 6 mm (¼ in) from edge. Take the faille side piece and turn in the seam allowance on the straight sides. Cut a piece of wadding [padding] slightly smaller than the faille. Place it behind the faille and sew the faille to the background. On the top of the cake, in pencil, very lightly trace 'Happy Birthday' onto the satin (**fig. 1**). Treat top in the same way as the side.

Working the embroidery

With couching stitch, using six strands of pink thread for the line and one strand for the tying stitch, embroider 'Happy Birthday'.

On the side of the cake mark the points of the scallops with small stitches or pencil dots (**fig. 1**). Embroider the scallops in couching stitch, using six strands and one strand of white embroidery thread.

Making the icing shells

Enlarge the design in **fig. 2** and lightly trace the 26 individual shells in pencil onto the medium lilac satin. Allow 2 cm (¾ in) all round each one. Cut out the first four shells. Stretch one of the 25 cm (10 in) squares of cotton fabric in the embroidery hoop.

With a piece of wadding [padding] under the satin, stitch each shell firmly to the cotton, all along the line, using a tiny back stitch and lilac sewing thread.

Cut close to the finished shapes and stitch each one onto the background. Repeat until all 26 shells have been sewn down.

Making the candles

Cut six strips of velvet ribbon, 6 cm (2⅜ in) long. Turn under 1 cm (⅜ in) at one end and sew on a piece of white stranded embroidery thread for the wick.

Fold over the ribbon, reducing the width to 1 cm (⅜ in) and stitch along the back. Sew each candle onto the background. Cut candle holders from white leather or felt and stitch over the bottom of the candles.

To finish

Baste the square of calico [unbleached cotton] to the back of the finished satin background square.

Sew the remaining two pieces of pale lilac satin together to make the back of the cushion cover, and insert the zipper in the seam.

With the zipper open and right sides together, sew front and back of the cushion cover together. Turn right side out. Sew white cord over the seam line. Insert the cushion pad [pillow form].

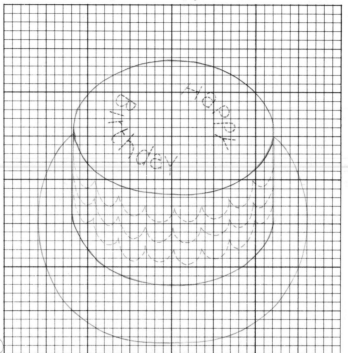

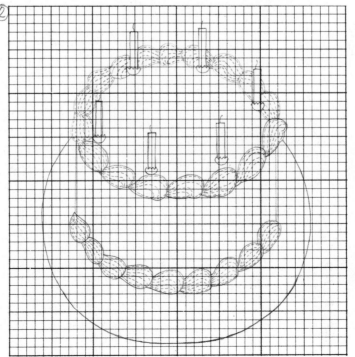

Appliqué picture

Finished size: 24 × 28 cm (9½ × 11 in)

MATERIALS

12 × 30 cm (5 × 12 in) pieces of satin in cream, pale green and purple/grey

Scraps of satin in dark green, blue, pink, orange, yellow and brown

36 cm (14 in) square of synthetic wadding [padding]

36 cm (14 in) square of calico [unbleached cotton] for backing

Machine embroidery thread in pink, purple, grey and green

Dressmakers' graph paper,

Tracing paper

Pencil

TO MAKE THE PICTURE

Enlarge the three designs (figs. 1, 2 and 3). Make tracings of the enlarged designs. From the cream satin, wadding [padding] and backing fabric cut pieces measuring 10 × 26 cm (4 × 10½ in).

From the pale green satin, wadding [padding] and backing fabric cut pieces measuring 11 × 26 cm (4½ × 10½ in). From the purple/grey satin, wadding [padding] and backing fabric cut pieces measuring 14 × 26 cm (5½ × 10½ in).

Lay each piece of backing fabric out and spread the wadding [padding] and satin on top. Pin each traced design centrally onto the satin: fig. 1 on the cream, fig. 2 on the green and fig. 3 on the purple/grey. Baste around the tracings, sewing through all three layers.

With any colour of thread in the sewing machine, lower the feed dog and, using the darning foot, work straight stitch through the tracings, following the design outlines carefully. Tear away the tracing paper, leaving the designs outlined by the stitching.

Working the appliqué and embroidery

Trace all the shapes to be appliquéd from the three parts of the design. In **fig. 1** all except the tree trunks are appliquéd.

In **fig. 2** the brown steps and in **fig. 3** the brown bricks are appliquéd.

Cut out the shapes and baste them to the satin backgrounds. Sew around each piece using a close zig-zag stitch and covering the raw edges of the satin. The remaining details are machine embroidered. The cars and flowers are worked in straight stitch, by solidly filling in the outlines using pink, purple and grey thread.

The tree trunks in **fig. 1** are worked in zig-zag stitch, as are the areas between the steps, flower stems and leaves in **fig. 2**.

To finish

Join the three parts of the picture together with a seam allowance of 1 cm (⅜ in). Make sure the designs match at points AB and CD.

The quilting may be stretched by pinning it face up to a piece of wood with a damp cloth between the wood and the quilting. First pin the centre of each side, then the corners, and so on. Leave for 24 hours.

The picture is now ready for framing.

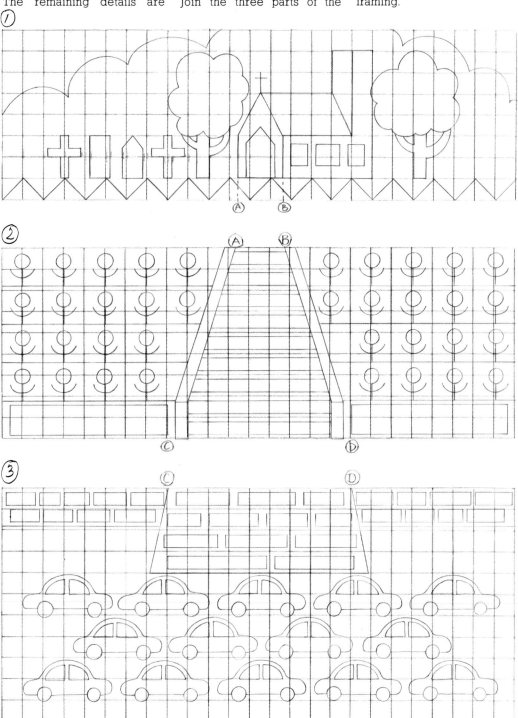

BABY'S JACKET
STRIPY QUILT

The satin baby's jacket is made up using a very quick and easy pattern. It illustrates how quilting can be used to 'paint' a picture. In contrast, the colourful stripy quilt needs careful planning and preparation before you begin. However – like so many good ideas – once the fabrics have been selected, it is wonderfully simple to make.

Baby's jacket

To fit: age 3–6 months

MATERIALS

0.5 m (½ yd) white washable satin, 115 cm (45 in) wide

0.5 m (½ yd) lightweight synthetic wadding [padding]

0.5 m (½ yd) light muslin, for backing

0.5 m (½ yd) white Viyella, 115 cm (45 in) wide

2 m (2¼ yd) green bias binding

Stranded embroidery thread in a selection of clear bright colours

Machine thread in white and green

Dressmakers' graph paper

Pencil

TO MAKE THE JACKET

Enlarge the pattern pieces in **fig. 1** onto the graph paper. (The pattern includes a 1 cm (⅜ in) seam allowance.) Cut out the pattern pieces in the satin, backing fabric and wadding [padding], allowing a little extra all round for shrinkage during quilting. Place the wadding [padding] between the satin and backing and secure with basting stitches.

Quilting the fabric

Follow the quilting design drawn on the pattern (**fig. 1**). Using two strands of embroidery thread in the colours of your choice, work the birds and the flowers as shown in **figs. 2** and **3**.

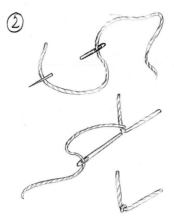

Work the remaining outlines in running stitch. Repeat the design on the two front jacket pieces.

When the quilting is complete, place the pieces on the paper pattern and trim to shape. Place the front pieces and back

piece right sides together and join shoulder seams. Trim away wadding [padding] from seam allowance and open flat. Using white embroidery thread, top stitch with a fine running stitch either side of the seam lines (**figs. 4** and **5**). Attach the basted sleeve pieces to the jacket. Trim the wadding [padding] and open out. Using emerald green embroidery thread, top stitch either side of the seam lines. Using the same colour thread, quilt the sleeves with parallel lines of running stitch, spaced 2.5 cm (1 in) apart (**fig. 4**).

To make up

Join the underarm seams, clipping into the corners under the arm. Join side seams. Trim seams; open out and top stitch with a fine running stitch in

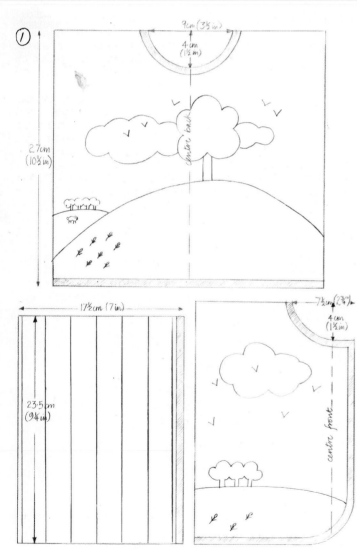

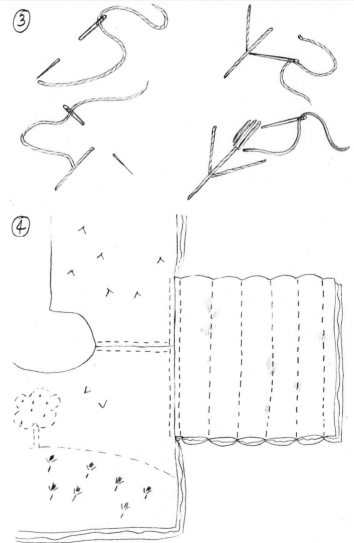

white embroidery thread, close to the seam lines.

Cut out the pattern in the Viyella lining fabric. Place right sides together and join seams. Trim and press. Leave the lining inside out and insert it into the jacket. Machine stitch around all edges and trim very close to stitching.

Bind all raw edges with green bias binding. Bind the bottom and front edges first, then the neck edge. Tuck in the ends of the binding at the front neck edge and hand stitch.

Sew on the heart-shaped buttons. To make the buttonholes, take several long stitches to make a loop which fits the button. Then make neat buttonhole stitches along the loop to finish (**fig. 6**).

Stripy quilt

Finished size: 244 cm (96 in) long, and either 183 cm (72 in) or 228 cm (90 in) wide.

MATERIALS

Strips of fabric either 185.5 cm (73 in) or 231 cm (91 in) long and of various widths

Either 5.60 m (6¼ yd) or 7 m (7½ yd) **light cotton fabric**, 90 cm (36 in) wide for backing

Synthetic wadding [padding] in the same quantity

Approximately 2.7 m (2¾ yd) **fabric**, 90 cm (36 in) wide for binding

Synthetic machine sewing thread to match backing fabric

Small adhesive labels

Tailors' chalk

Long ruler

TO MAKE THE QUILT
Preparing the fabric

The quilt is made up in three sections to avoid manipulating a great bulk. Each section is backed with a length of 90 cm (36 in) wide fabric. Allowing for seams, this will produce a measurement of 266 cm (105 in) from top to bottom of the quilt. With quilting this will contract to the finished length of 244 cm (96 in).

The strips of fabric should therefore total 266 cm (105 in) plus a seam allowance of 1.5 cm (⅝ in) on each side of each strip. Different kinds of fabric can be mixed successfully and the widths of the strips can be varied. Include about 15 to 20 different fabrics. Choose a colour range and include fabrics such as good quality print and plain cottons, wool and soft synthetics (woven not knitted). Pants, long skirts and dresses can be cut up and used.

Cut or tear long pieces of fabric to the width required along the grain, and then join them together to make strips long enough for the width of the finished quilt.

Arrange the strips in the order you want, number them with the adhesive labels and pin them together in order.

Sewing the quilt

Cut backing and wadding [padding] each into three equal pieces and make up each section of the quilt separately. Lay the backing on the wadding [padding]. Pin and baste round the edges and down the middle, and then at 15 cm (6 in) intervals along the length. Measure and mark each line accurately first with the tailors' chalk. Be sure that the stitches can be seen from the wadding [padding] side as they will form the guidelines for sewing the strips to the backing.

Lay the backing section out with the wadding [padding] on top. Place the first strip face up along the top edge of the wadding, so the edge of the backing just shows around three sides. Place the second strip face down on the first, with the bottom edge of the first strip showing 3 mm (⅛ in) below the second (**fig. 1**). Pin about every 7.5 cm (3 in), 6 mm (¼ in) from the edge of the upper strip and then machine stitch, removing pins as you go. Turn the second strip face upwards and repeat with the third strip and so on to complete the first section of the quilt.

When working the sections, make sure that the pins go right through to the backing, that the backing does not pucker and the strips remain parallel to the basted guidelines.

You can sew extra quilting lines along the wider strips if you wish.

To finish

Make all three sections in the same way, then join up the quilt. Pin and seam the fabric strips together (**fig. 2**). Trim away any surplus wadding [padding], then slip stitch the backing together, turning in the raw edges.

With a few pins placed crosswise, machine stitch along the top seam.

Trim the edges of the quilt.

The width of the binding can be adjusted to give you exact final measurements. Cut binding strips to double the width required plus 3 cm (1¼ in) to allow for turnings of 1.5 cm (⅝ in). Cut two strips the length of the sides and two for top and bottom.

Starting with one side, machine stitch binding to quilt, right sides facing, without stretching the quilting. Turn binding over, turn in raw edges and hem to the backing.

Repeat for the other side then for top and bottom.

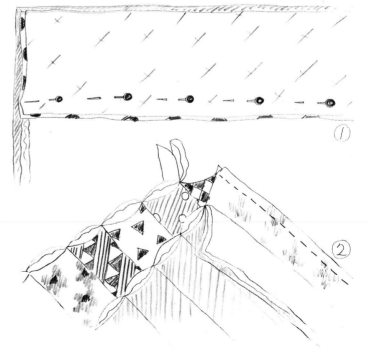

CHRISTENING QUILT
QUILTED CHAIR COVER

The detail of the Christening quilt, below, shows the lovely effects which can be produced by spray-dyeing materials using a mouth spray diffuser. The equipment required can be obtained through all good art shops.

To make the Suffolk puff [yo-yo] patches – which are part of the chair seat design – you will need to prepare circular templates from stiff paper or fine card [cardboard]. The finished puffs will be slightly less than half the diameter of the template. Place and pin the template onto the wrong side of the fabric. Cut out the fabric 6 mm (¼ in) larger all round than the template. Turn the extra fabric onto the wrong side. Using strong thread – secured by back stitches – work evenly spaced running stitches 3 mm (⅛ in) from the edge through the double material. To complete the patch, gather the edges into the centre.

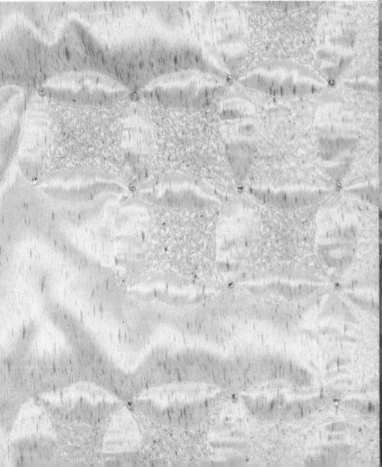

Christening quilt

Finished size: 100 × 145 cm (39 × 57 in)

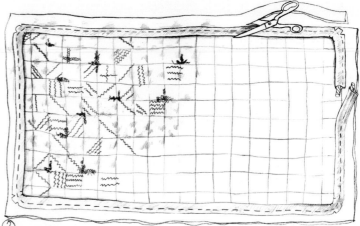

MATERIALS

5 m (5½ yd) white satin, 90 cm (36 in) wide

3 m (3¼ yd) synthetic wadding [padding]

3 m (3¼ yd) calico [unbleached cotton] for lining

3 m (3¼ yd) piping, covered with cotton floral print

1 packet clear glass beads

Synthetic machine thread (2 shades blue, 2 shades pink, 1 pale purple, 3 shades green, white)

Tracing paper

Pencil

Ruler

TO MAKE THE QUILT

Begin work on the centre piece.

Cut out satin, wadding [padding] and lining, each a generous 65 × 110 cm (26 × 44 in) to allow for shrinkage.

Draw a rectangle 50 × 95 cm (20 × 38 in) on tracing paper, and divide this into 5 cm (2 in) squares.

Baste paper to the fabric, wadding [padding] and lining working out from the centre.

Machine stitch along traced lines through the paper using straight stitch and the zig-zag foot; again work from the centre outwards.

Working the pattern

Remove tracing paper and trim wadding [padding]. Decorate squares as shown (**fig. 1**). Using zig-zag stitch, work patterns in alternate squares, varying colours of the threads.

Occasionally, where lines join, make a series of tailor tacks using tailor tacking foot and three shades of green thread (see photograph of quilt).

Neaten wrong side of quilt and remove basting stitches. Pin and baste the covered piping around the edge of the centre piece (**fig. 2**).

Preparing the borders

Cut satin, wadding [padding] and lining for border pieces: 2 strips 155 × 28 cm (61 × 11 in) and 2 strips 110 × 28 cm (43 × 11 in). (Measurements include seam allowances.) Trim the ends making 45° angles (**fig. 3**). Make a trace pattern of intersecting circles 5 cm (2 in) in diameter, using a jar lid or compasses. Baste paper to fabrics, working from centre outwards. Machine stitch around circles using straight stitch and the darning foot.

Remove tracing paper and work free machine stitch or zig-zag stitch (**figs. 4** and **5**) in the circles with white and green thread. Where circles intersect sew a glass bead.

Repeat for each of the four border pieces.

Optional Make up a mixture of dyes and inks in pink and green. With a mouth spray diffuser, spray each colour separately, first pink then green, onto each border piece.

To finish

Sew border pieces to the centre piece. Slip stitch edges of border pieces together.

Optional Make up an extra 6 m (6½ yd) of satin-covered piping; pin and baste to outer edge of quilt.

Make the backing with the remaining satin. The backing will need a centre seam as the satin is not wide enough to cover the whole quilt. Cut the backing large enough to leave a generous seam allowance around the quilt. With right sides facing, sew quilt to backing, leaving one small side open. Turn quilt the right way and slip stitch opening.

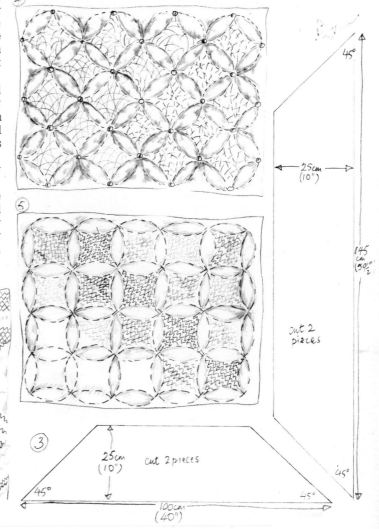

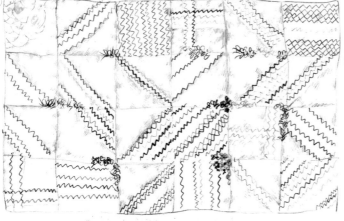

Quilted chair cover

MATERIALS

2 m (2¼ yd) close woven furnishing fabric, 122 cm (48 in) wide

46 × 114 cm (18 × 45 in) synthetic wadding

46 cm (18 in) calico (unbleached cotton), 90 cm (36 in) wide

Small piece of green cotton print fabric

46 cm (18 in) iron-on interfacing

Cream buttonhole thread

Cream sewing thread

Stranded embroidery thread in green

Bouclé (or any other novelty knobbly knitting yarn) in green

6 cm (2½ in) diameter circular template for Suffolk puff (yo-yo) patches

Dressmakers' graph paper

Tracing paper

Pencil

TO MAKE THE CHAIR COVER

The quantities and measurements given are for covering a simple metal frame chair 36 cm (14 in) wide. Paint the chair frame first to tone with the colours of the quilted cover. Cut two pieces of furnishing fabric 39.5 × 104 cm (15½ × 41 in). This includes allowance for 2 cm (¾ in) seams. Put one piece aside for backing. Also cut one strip of furnishing fabric 7.5 × 30 cm (3 × 12 in) and put this aside.

Copy the design (**fig. 1**) and trace it full size onto the tracing paper. Make separate tracings of the path, houses and sheaves of corn. Baste the full size design centrally to the piece of furnishing fabric then tear the paper away leaving the design outlined in stitches.

Iron the interfacing to the calico [unbleached cotton] and cut out the path, house and corn shapes using the tracing paper patterns. Sew these in place on the background using straight machine stitch.

Embroider the details of the houses using three strands of embroidery thread.

Baste the wadding [padding] to the back of the furnishing fabric and stitch all the quilting lines using straight machine stitch and buttonhole thread.

Couch down the novelty knitting yarn for the hedgerows using one strand of embroidery thread.

Make about 25 Suffolk puff [yo-yo] patches from the green print fabric (**fig. 2**) and sew them in place, as shown in the diagram.

Fitting the chair cover

Take the piece of furnishing fabric reserved for the backing and measure 50 cm (20 in) down one long side. Sew the 30 cm (12 in) strip of fabric centrally to the backing at this point along one side only. The free side of the strip will be sewn over the central bar at the back of the chair seat.

Sew the backing to the quilted fabric. With right sides together, machine stitch all around the pieces, 2 cm (¾ in) from the edge, leaving a section open along the top to pull the fabric through to the right side.

Turn right side out and oversew the opening, turning in raw edges.

Cut two pieces of furnishing fabric the same size as the pieces of canvas on the chair, plus extra for turning under the raw edges, and make replacement seat and backrest pieces. The chair will look more attractive from the back if it is covered all in one fabric.

Lay the quilted fabric over the chair and attach the centre strip to the central bar of the chair and sew it down with strong thread (**fig. 3a**). Sew the top and bottom of the quilting over the top and bottom bars of the chair (**figs. 3b** and **3c**), stitching firmly by hand.

Details of how to make Suffolk puff [yo-yo] patches are given on page 46.

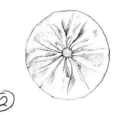

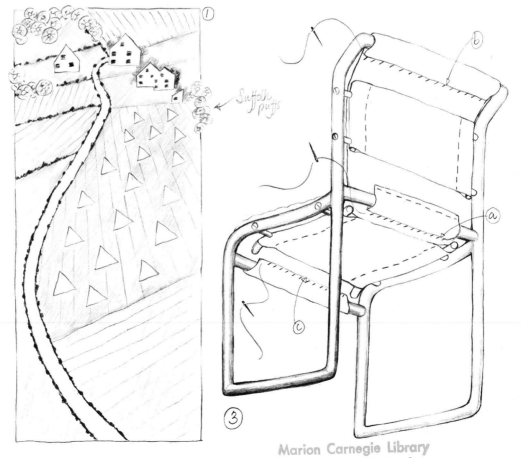

MAN'S WAISTCOAT [VEST]

DAFFODIL WAISTCOAT [VEST]

The leaf pattern on the man's quilted waistcoat [vest] and the flower centres and surrounding areas on the woman's jacket are embroidered with clusters of French knots. These are formed by twisting the embroidery thread on the surface of the fabric and securing with a stitch. To do this, first draw the thread through to the right side of the fabric, then twist the needle two or three times around the thread and insert it back into the same hole. This leaves a raised knot on the surface of the work. French knots form a very effective relief pattern in the centre of flower motifs. They are also often used to create sprinkled or dotted effects – as on the daffodil design.

Man's waistcoat [vest]

To fit: chest size 97 cm (38 in), waist size 82 cm (32 in)

MATERIALS

2.25 m (2½ yd) polyester satin crepe, 112 cm (44 in) wide

1 m (39 in) light muslin, 90 cm (36 in) wide, for backing

64 cm (25 in) non-woven interfacing

1 m (39 in) medium weight synthetic wadding [padding], 90 cm (36 in) wide

Synthetic sewing thread to match main fabric

5 covered buttons

Buckle for belt

Dressmakers' graph paper

Tracing paper

Pencil

TO MAKE THE WAISTCOAT

Making the pattern

Enlarge pattern pieces (**fig. 1**) onto the graph paper and draw quilting design onto front and back pieces.

Make tracings of pattern front and back, then reverse the tracings and make second tracings of the facing sides so you have tracings of two fronts and two backs.

Preparing the fabric

Pin tracings to main fabric. To allow for drawing in of fabric during quilting, leave a generous margin of fabric, about 5 to 7.5 cm (2 to 3 in) all around, then cut out a rectangle of fabric for each pattern piece. Do not cut round outline of pattern.

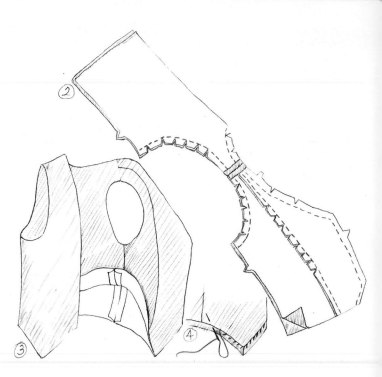

Baste around outline of pattern to mark shape on the fabric.

Stitch around design outlines with small running stitch. Gently tear tracing paper away from the fabric.

Cut wadding [padding] and backing to same size as top fabric. Spread out backing, and place wadding [padding] and satin crepe on top. Pin all three layers together at the edges. Starting at the centre, baste layers together in horizontal and vertical lines. Leave thread loose at the end of each line.

Quilting the fabric

Using the matching sewing thread, outline all leaves and stalks on fronts with back stitch.

Work leaf veins in chain stitch, graduating the size of the stitches so they are smaller towards leaf edges.

Make clusters of French knots in each leaf.

Work quilting for the back pieces entirely in back stitch. Work from centre outwards.

To make up

Cut out the quilted pattern pieces, allowing 1.5 cm (⅝ in) all round for seams.

In the remaining satin cut out two of the back piece; trace the two sections of the front piece

① (diagram labels) Back / interfacing / Front / Belt position / lining / Left back belt (cut one) / Right back belt (cut one)

(divide along dotted lines) and cut two of each. Cut the interfacing also in the interfacing fabric. Add 1.5 cm (⅝ in) seam allowance to all edges.

Pin interfacing to wrong sides of fronts. Cut corner of interfacing to about 6 mm (¼ in). Baste. Before stitching seams, cut back wadding [padding] 1.5 cm (⅝ in) to avoid a bulky seam.

Stitch centre back seam, ensuring that quilting patterns are symmetrical.

Fold right back belt and left back belt lengthwise, right sides together. Stitch, leaving short ends near notches free. Trim corners diagonally. Trim seam allowance. Turn right side out and press.

Baste right back belt to back at right side, and left back belt to back at left side.

Stitch back to fronts at shoulders.

Trim interfacing close to stitching.

Sewing the lining

For lining stay stitch inward curves on front facing 12 mm (½ in). Clip curve. Stitch front facing to front lining, right sides together. Press seam towards armhole.

Stitch centre back seam in back lining.

Stitch back lining to front facings and linings at shoulders. Pin linings and facings to quilted pieces, right sides together. Stitch neck, front and armhole edges together. Cut corners diagonally; trim seam allowance. Clip curves (fig. 2).

Turn right side out, pulling fronts through shoulders towards back.

With right sides together, pin front to back at sides. Pin front lining to back lining and stitch entire seam.

Turn right side out (fig. 3). Slip stitch lower edges together (fig. 4). Press lower edge gently with warm iron.

To finish

Make worked buttonholes at positions indicated on left front. Mark and sew buttons under buttonholes. Slip buckle through left back belt and sew in place.

Daffodil waistcoat [vest]

MATERIALS

Bought pattern for sleeveless jacket or waistcoat [vest]

Stretch knit jersey fabric, quantity as given on pattern

Synthetic wadding [padding] and lining fabrics in similar quantities

Stranded embroidery thread

Matching sewing thread

Tissue paper

Pencil

TO MAKE THE JACKET

Cut out jacket and lining fabric following pattern instructions, and allowing a little extra all round for shrinkage in quilting. Place a layer of wadding [padding] between fabric and lining and secure with basting. Machine stitch darts and side seams, according to pattern instructions, leaving shoulder seams open (fig. 1).

Trace flower motifs (fig. 2) onto tissue paper. Position tissue paper on jacket, using fig. 1 as a guide.

Baste through all layers, then tear away paper, leaving design outlined in stitches.

Quilting the fabric

Work flower outlines in back stitch using two strands of embroidery thread. Work French knots in flower centres and between vertical lines (fig. 3).

Baste the vertical lines of the design on the jacket using photograph on page 50 as a guide. Machine stitch along the lines using both straight stitch and zig-zag stitching in various widths (fig. 3). All stitching must be worked in the same direction (from top to hem) to prevent the fabric wrinkling.

Machine stitch shoulder seams. Bind armholes and outer edge with fabric strips.

If buttons are required, make loops of fabric instead of working buttonholes.

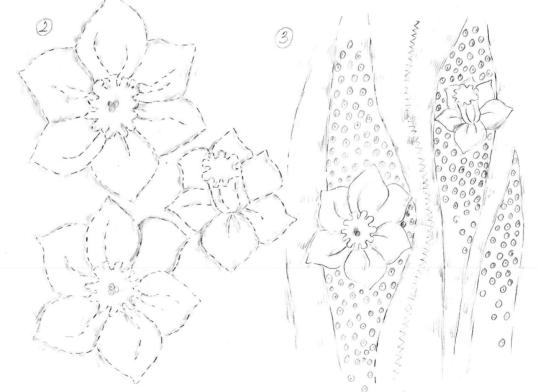

SILK JACKET WITH RUCHED SLEEVES

It is the finishing touches on this beautiful silk jacket which make it so special. The sleeves are lined in bright pink and the seams finished with colourful piping and tassels. The selection of the coloured silks used for covering the piping and making the tassels is left to your personal choice. The body of the jacket is lined in red silk, but another strong colour could be used if

preferred. Before you begin, select your colours carefully and arrange them on the red silk until you find the effect which is most pleasing to you.

The jacket in the photograph was made up in dupion – a handwoven Indian silk. For the silk to hang correctly it is essential that it is cut on the grain, as indicated on the diagram for the pattern pieces.

This is a relatively advanced project for experienced dressmakers.

Silk jacket with ruched sleeves

To fit: bust size 86–91 cm (34–36 in)

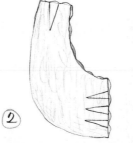

②

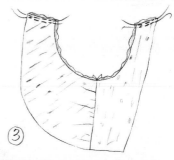

③

MATERIALS

2.5 m (2⅔ yd) red wild [raw] silk, 90 cm (36 in) wide

1 m (39 in) pink silk lining fabric, 90 cm (36 in) wide for sleeve lining

2 m (2¼ yd) lightweight synthetic wadding [padding], 90 cm (36 in) wide

50 cm (20 in) lengths of silk in various colours for tassels and piping

6 m (6½ yd) fine piping cord, for exterior piping

165 cm (65 in) very fine piping cord, for inside jacket

Matching sewing thread

Dressmakers' graph paper

Pencil

TO MAKE THE JACKET

Cutting out the jacket

Enlarge the pattern pieces (fig. 1) onto the graph paper and cut them out.

In the main fabric – folded double – cut out the pattern pieces (except for the tassels), cutting four each of the jacket front, side back panel and front band and two each of the other pieces. Align the arrows with the lengthwise grain of the fabric. Mark the sleeve sections with tailor tacks to indicate the areas to be gathered. Also mark the back sleeve pieces for easy identification. Trim one of the centre backs along the lines indicated by the dashes on the pattern to form the lining piece. A seam allowance of 1.5 cm (⅝ in) is included. Stay stitch around the edges of the front panels and band pieces, and zig-zag stitch around the edges of the other pieces to prevent fraying. Cut the pieces in the wadding [padding]: one piece each of the centre back panel and back band; two each of the remaining pieces.

From the pink lining fabric – folded – cut two pieces each of the front and back sleeve sections, as indicated on the cutting layout.

Preparing the tassels

Cut the tassel pieces – any number you like – from different coloured silks, cutting them against the grain [crosswise] as indicated. Fold each strip in half lengthwise, right sides facing, and stitch along the edge and across one end. Trim seam, turn and press.

Preparing the piping

Cover the very fine piping cord with strips of the main fabric, 2.5 cm (1 in) wide, cut on the bias and joined with diagonal seams. Cover the other cord with strips of coloured silk.

Assembling the jacket

Make two rows of gathering stitches on the straight sides of all four front pieces. Put two of them aside for the lining. Draw up the gathers along the longer (side) edge until it matches the corresponding edge on the side back.

Make rows of gathering on the shoulder edges of the side back pieces, but do not draw them up. Put two pieces aside for the lining. Pin and stitch darts in the wadding [padding] front sections at sides, so that they fit the front side edges. Also dart the shoulder edges so that they measure 9 cm (3½ in)

(fig. 2). Pin and baste the wadding [padding] pieces to the wrong sides of the fronts and side backs, except at shoulders.

Pin, baste and stitch the fronts and side backs together, right sides facing, at the side seams only (fig. 3). Press seams open. Working with a right and left band piece and one back band piece, baste the corresponding wadding [padding] pieces to the wrong sides. Stitch the band sections together at the side seams only, as shown in

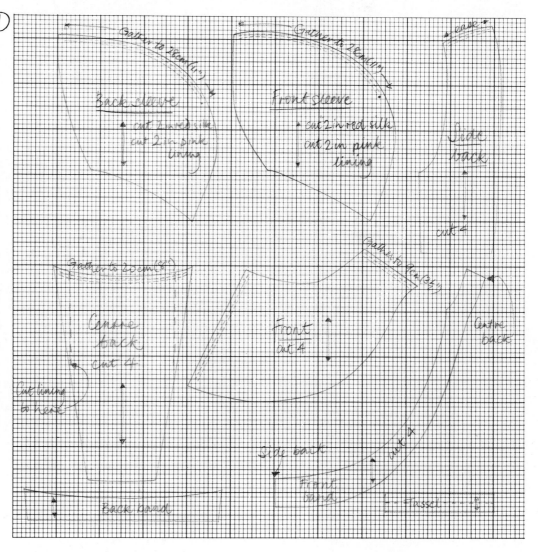

①

Back sleeve
· cut 2 in red silk
cut 2 in pink lining

Gather to 28 cm (11 in)

Front sleeve
· cut 2 in red silk
cut 2 in pink lining

Gather to 28 cm (11 in)

Side back

cut 4

Gather to 20 cm (8 in)

Centre back
cut 4

Gather to 9 cm (3½)

Front
cut 4

Centre back

Cut lining to here

Side back

Front band

Back band

Tassel

fig. 4. Press the seams open.
Pin a length of multicoloured piping to front edge of each front-side back section, matching raw edges. Place the band on top, right side down, matching inner edge of band to outer edges of main sections (**fig. 5**). Baste and stitch close to piping, and ending stitching 7.5 cm (3 in) from edge of side back to allow for insertion later of centre back. Trim seams, trimming wadding [padding] very close to stitching.

Stitch remaining three band sections together to make band lining. Pin a length of multicoloured piping along entire outer edge of band, matching raw edges. Pin band lining along this edge, right sides facing. Baste and stitch close to piping (**fig. 6**). Trim seam, trimming wadding [padding] close to stitching. Turn band lining to inside. Baste through the band layers close to piping to push piping to edge. Press lightly and remove basting.

Pin and baste sleeve wadding [padding] sections to wrong sides of four sleeve pieces. Join underarm seams of sleeves (**fig. 7**) and linings.

Make two rows of gathering stitches along the upper edge of each sleeve section, including wadding [padding], and each lining section.

Cut two lengths of contrast piping, each 95 cm (37 in) long. On each sleeve, pin the piping to the right side, matching raw edges, between the areas to be gathered, leaving the remaining length of piping free at one end. Pin and baste the lining to the sleeve along the piped edge (**fig. 8**). Stitch. Trim seam, turn sleeve right side out, baste along edges, press lightly and remove basting.

Pin sleeves into jacket armholes, leaving lining free and matching underarm to side seams (**fig. 9**).

Pin tassels near ends of seam, varying their lengths slightly. Baste and stitch. Trim seams, clip curves and press seams towards sleeve. Trim away excess on tassels.

Gather up front lining pieces at sides to fit side back linings. Pin and baste side edges together, right sides facing, inserting red

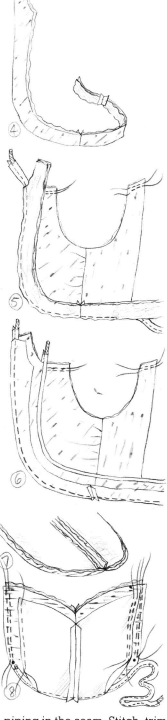

piping in the seam. Stitch, trim and press.

Pin, baste and stitch the front-side back lining sections to the free edge of the band lining, right sides facing, leaving 7.5 cm (3 in) unstitched on backs. Clip curves, trim seam and press. Pin, baste and stitch sleeve linings to front-side back linings, right sides facing. Trim, clip curves and press seam allowances towards

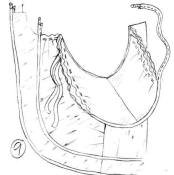

sleeve. Turn right side out. Make two rows of gathering on upper edges of centre back and centre back lining. Pull up gathers, on main piece only, to measure 20 cm (8 in). Dart wadding [padding] piece to match (**fig. 10**) and baste it to wrong side of main piece. Join centre back to side backs, inserting multicoloured piping in the seams. Press. Stitch lower edge to back band. Press. Join centre back lining to side back linings, inserting red piping in the seams. Press. Join lower edge to band lining. Press. Pull up gathers on sleeve sections (excluding linings) to measure 28 cm (11 in). Gather up shoulder edges on fronts and side backs (excluding linings) to measure 9 cm (3½ in) (**fig. 11**). Pin the entire upper arm-shoulder seam together, inserting the free length of piping (**fig. 12**). Stitch seam, clip curves and press open.

Draw up the gathers on sleeve linings and join sleeve lining seams. Press open.

Pin continuations of band to gathered back neck edge, including wadding [padding]. Stitch band and band lining ends together where they meet at the centre. Trim excess and press seam open. Baste and stitch centre back to band (**fig. 13**). Press.

Draw up gathers on lining shoulder edges to fit outer shoulder seam. Fold front shoulder seam allowances over back and insert short lengths of red piping under the fold. Hand stitch the seams. Draw up gathers on centre back lining. Fold the edge of the band lining over the gathered edge and hand stitch in place (**fig. 14**).

Decorate the band with two rows of machine stitching.

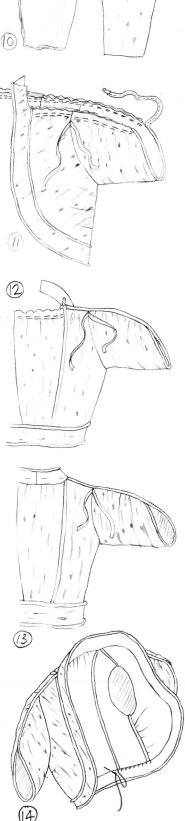

QUILTED CIRÉ COAT
CHEVRON JACKET

The teenager's quilted coat is made up in a ciré fabric, but most cottons and other closely woven fabrics would be suitable. A soft, openweave cotton lining fabric and a terylene wadding [padding] are other recommended materials for this pattern. The diagram (**fig. 1**, page 60) shows the complete cutting layout for the pattern pieces.
The pretty sleeveless jacket is another very useful lightweight garment, which is comfortable and easy to wear. For the chevron quilting design to be worked effectively, the main fabric must have a small, evenly spaced repeating pattern.

Quilted ciré coat

To fit: ages 12–14	12	13	14
Chest	78 cm (30 in)	82 cm (32 in)	86 cm (34 in)
Back neck–hem	94 cm (37 in)	100 cm (39 in)	106 cm (41 in)
Neck–wrist	58 cm (23 in)	60 cm (24 in)	64 cm (25 in)

MATERIALS

Ciré fabric, 150 cm (58 in) wide	1.90 m (2 yd)	1.90 m (2 yd)	2 m (2¼ yd)
Lining fabric, 90 cm (36 in) wide	2.40 m (2½ yd)	2.40 m (2½ yd)	2.50 m (2⅔ yd)
Polyester wadding [padding], 100 cm (39 in) wide	3.20 m (3½ yd)	3.20 m (3½ yd)	3.30 m (3⅔ yd)

6 matching buttons

2 reels synthetic thread

Dressmakers' graph paper

Felt tip pen

TO MAKE THE COAT

Enlarge the pattern pieces from the cutting layout (fig. 1). From all fabrics cut out one back, pair of fronts, pair of sleeves, pair of pockets.

From main fabric cut one pair of front bands, pair of wrist bands, one hem band, one neck band, pair of pocket bands. Also cut these out in wadding [padding] but to half their width.

Seam allowance is 1.5 cm (⅝ in) unless otherwise specified.

Quilting the pieces

Avoid putting pins into ciré except around edges, as they leave permanent holes.

Slightly loosen presser foot and work all the quilting lines with a large machine stitch.

Start with the fronts. Pin ciré right side up to wadding [padding] around edges. Sew from neck to hem along centre front, 1 cm (⅜ in) from edge. Make first quilting line 6.5 cm (2½ in) from centre front edge.

Use a tape measure and measure as you go. Sew a short length; move tape measure down, and continue stitching in short lengths to end. Smooth fabric before stitching next line.

Continue quilting lines parallel to the first, 5 cm (2 in) apart. Sew all quilting lines in one direction, from top to bottom, otherwise fabric will be distorted.

To quilt the sleeves, pin ciré to wadding [padding], fold through shoulder notch and centre wrist to form crease, marking first quilting line. Sew next lines 5 cm (2 in) on either side of centre quilting line and continue across sleeve.

Begin quilting back by folding along centre back line and working quilting lines 5 cm (2 in) apart.

To quilt the pockets, work two lines of stitching 6.5 cm (2½ in) from edges, 5 cm (2 in) apart.

Join wadding [padding] to bands by stitching lengthwise to one side of centre fold line.

To make the bands

Place one end of neck band on front bands and trim one end of each front band to match angle on neck band.

Place each front band right side up on wadding [padding] piece; pin and stitch with ciré on top, stitching 6 mm (¼ in) outside seam line on long edges (fig. 2). Also attach wadding [padding] to neck band.

Place one end of neck band, right sides together, on trimmed end of one front band. Pin and stitch pointed ends, starting and finishing 1.5 cm (⅝ in) from edge (fig. 3). Double stitch point and trim seam allowance close at point.

Press seam open, push out corner and fold band wrong sides together, forming mitred front corner.

Stitch other neck band corner, and join lower ends of front bands to hem band in the same way so that, when completed, band is in one continuous length.

Pin wadding [padding] to wrong sides of wrist bands and join each into a ring.

Sleeves

Join underarm seams, press seam allowance to front and top stitch 6 mm (¼ in) from seam.

Join underarm seams on lining, press seams open.

Put sleeve lining into sleeve, wrong sides together, and sew together, 6 mm (¼ in) from edge, around wrist.

Pin wadded wrist band to wrist edge of sleeve, rights sides together, matching join to underarm seam, and stitch.

Turn sleeve wrong side out; press seam allowance under band. Press seam allowance on

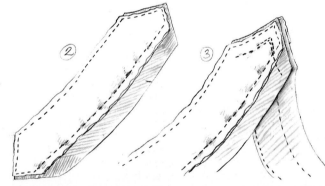

② ③

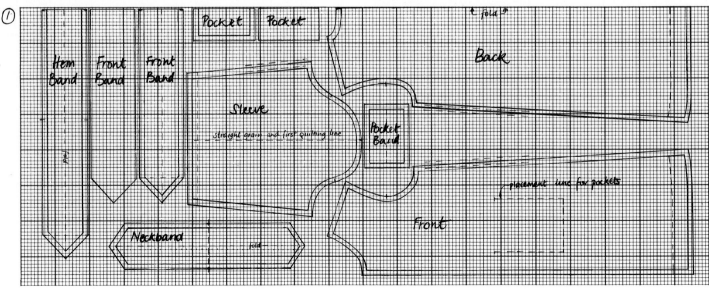

free edge of band over to wrong side, pin and slip stitch along first stitching line.

Pockets

Place lining on wrong side of pockets; stitch around edges. Place unstitched edge of band on edge of pocket, right sides together; pin, stitch and press seam allowance under band. Press seam allowance on free edge of band to wrong side and pin along first stitching line, turning under raw edges. Slip stitch in place.

To make up

Join fronts to back along side and shoulder seams. Press seam allowance towards back; top stitch 6 mm (¼ in) from seam. Join side and shoulder seams on lining; press seams open. Place lining in coat, wrong sides together. Pin and stitch around armholes, hem, neck and left front. Leave lining free on right front.
Set in sleeves, matching sleeve notch to shoulder seam, underarm to side seam and back and front notches. Press seam allowance towards sleeve. Bring lining up and pin and slip stitch in place over armhole seam.

Attaching the bands

Place unsewn edge of neck band on neck edge, right sides together, matching centre of band to centre back. Pin and stitch.
Place left front band on left front, right sides together. Pin and stitch.
Place hem band on hem, right sides together. Pin and stitch.
Place right front band on right front, right sides together. Pin and stitch, leaving lining free, between buttonholes and down to hem.
Press seam allowance under bands, except on right front. On this press seam open to form buttonholes and press seam allowance on right front lining to wrong side and pin and slip stitch close to centre front.
Press seam allowance on free quilted edge of band to wrong side and pin in place along first stitching line. Slip stitch and make stay stitches at each end of buttonholes as you go. Sew on buttons.

Chevron jacket

To fit: bust size approx. 92 cm (36 in)

MATERIALS

1.5 m (1⅝ yd) fabric, 90 cm (36 in) wide with small repeating pattern

1.5 m (1⅝ yd) toning lining fabric, 90 cm (36 in) wide

1.5 m (1⅝ yd) synthetic wadding [padding], 90 cm (36 in) wide

Small piece iron-on interfacing

Matching sewing thread

Contrasting sewing thread

Small buckle

5 hammer-in snap fasteners

Dressmakers' graph paper

Pencil

TO MAKE THE JACKET

Enlarge pattern pieces (fig. 1). Cut out pieces A and B in main fabric and wadding [padding], allowing extra 4 cm (1½ in) all around for shrinkage.
Cut out lining very slightly smaller all around than the pattern.
Pin main fabric to wadding [padding], starting from the centre of each piece. Starting from the centre of each piece, work quilting by machine stitching in a chevron pattern and using the contrasting thread.
Work the first line of quilting and then use quilting guide foot to work remaining lines.
Replace pattern on finished quilted pieces and trim away

the excess fabric to fit.
Cut out belt straps and iron interfacing onto wrong side. Fold lengthwise with right sides together. Stitch long side and one short side. Trim, turn right side out and press.
Stitch to jacket back as shown (fig. 2).
Join shoulder seams on quilted pieces. Trim away excess wadding [padding] from seam allowances.

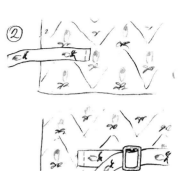

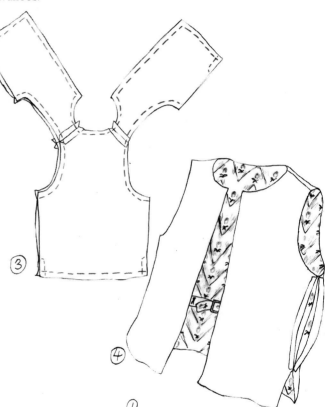

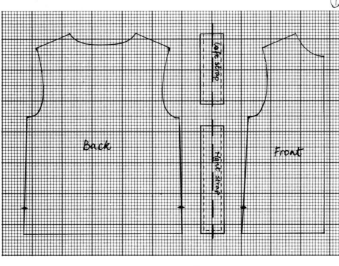

Join shoulder seams on lining. With right sides together, stitch lining to quilted pieces, leaving side seams open except for bottom 7.5 cm (3 in) (fig. 3). Trim and turn to right side.
Join side seams of quilted pieces with right sides together, leaving lining free (fig. 4). Trim.
Turn in seam allowances of lining and slip stitch together. Top stitch around jacket along the edges: once close to the edge and a second round 1 cm (⅜ in) away.
Fix five hammer-in snap fasteners down front.

SLIPPER BOOTS
'RISING SUN' WALL HANGING

Here are two bright and colourful projects designed for children. The slipper boots are ideal for children to wear about the house. They are made in cotton with a felt sole.

For a more hardwearing slipper, the soles could be made up in a soft leather. The diagram (**fig. 1**, page 65) shows the complete cutting layout for the pattern pieces. The quilting lines have also been marked for guidance.

The wall hanging makes a bright splash of colour for a child's bedroom or playroom. The small toadstools, blades of grass and daisies are embroidered in satin stitch.

'Rising Sun' wall hanging

Finished size: 57 × 72 cm (22½ × 28½ in)

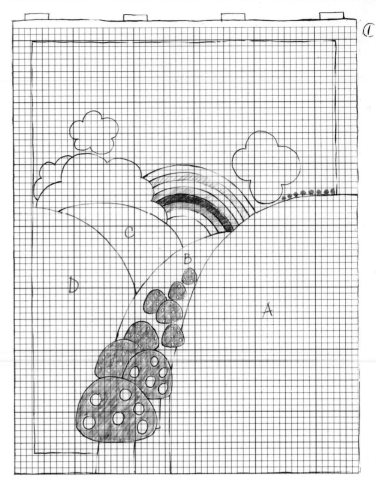

MATERIALS

1 m (39 in) white cotton, 120 cm (48 in) wide

40 cm (16 in) sky blue cotton, 90 cm (36 in) wide

50 cm (20 in) green satin, 90 cm (36 in) wide

1.4 m (55 in) medium weight interfacing, 90 cm (36 in) wide

76 cm (30 in) synthetic wadding [padding], 90 cm (36 in) wide

10 cm (4 in) square of white felt

Scraps of red cotton fabric for toadstools

Scraps of yellow, marigold, orange, rust, mauve, brown, red and sky blue cotton fabric for sun

Stranded embroidery thread in red, white, green, yellow and blue

Sewing cotton in white, sky blue and brown

Dressmakers' graph paper

Black felt tip pen

Pencil

56 cm (22 in) length of dowel

TO MAKE THE WALL HANGING

Enlarge the design (**fig. 1**) onto graph paper and outline in felt tip pen.

Cut a piece of interfacing 59 × 76 cm (23¼ × 30 in) for backing the hanging and put aside.

On remainder of interfacing, trace in pencil the clouds, the sun shapes, fields and toadstools. Cut the pieces out and use them as templates.

Cutting out the fabric

From the white cotton, cut two pieces 59 × 76 cm (23¼ × 30 in) and four pieces 10 cm (4 in) square.

From the sky blue cotton cut one piece 40 × 52 cm (16 × 20½ in).

Using templates as guides, cut out field pieces from green satin, adding 1 cm (⅜ in) all round.

Cut out clouds, toadstools and sun pieces, adding 6 mm (¼ in) all round and using appropriate coloured fabrics. Make sure that the straight grain of the fabric will run vertically on each piece when it is attached. Cut out toadstool stems and spots from white felt.

Cut a piece of wadding [padding] 59 × 76 cm (23¼ × 30 in).

Working the design

Turn in 1.5 cm (⅝ in) along the top and sides of the sky piece and stitch in place on one 59 × 76 cm (23¼ × 30 in) piece white cotton background.

Turn in 6 mm (¼ in) on top curve of each sun piece and, starting with outer blue piece, sew each colour to the one above. Finally sew the completed sun in place in the sky.

Baste interfacing template to the back of each cloud, sandwiching a little wadding [padding] in between. Snip curves where necessary, turn fabric over the interfacing and baste in position (**fig. 2**). Leave unturned the parts that will be overlapped by other pieces of fabric, and stitch clouds onto sky.

For the fields, turn in 1.5 cm (⅝ in), except on the straight edges of pieces A and B and where B, C and D are overlapped. Sew C, B, D and A onto background.

Make the toadstools in the same way as the clouds and sew in place, adding felt stems and spots.

Finally, using two strands of thread, embroider small toadstools, grass and daisies in satin stitch and straight stitches as shown (**fig. 3**).

To finish

Pin the piece of wadding [padding] to the back of the hanging and sew in place with concealed stitches around the edge of clouds, sun and hills.

Fold and sew the four pieces of white cotton fabric to make four tubes, with a seam allowance of 1 cm (⅜ in). Turn right side out and press flat. Fold each in half crosswise and pin it to top edge of hanging with loops facing inwards. Baste in place.

With right sides together, place remaining piece of white cotton on the hanging with a layer of interfacing on top. Baste and stitch these layers together, 1.5 cm (⅝ in) from the edge. Leave 30 cm (12 in) unstitched along one side. Turn right side out, and slip stitch the opening.

Slide dowel rod through the loops.

Slipper boots

To fit a foot 16 cm (6½ in) long

MATERIALS

30 cm (12 in) cotton fabric, 90 cm (36 in) wide for boots

30 cm (12 in) cotton fabric, 90 cm (36 in) wide for lining

60 cm (24 in) cotton fabric, 90 cm (36 in) wide for bias strips

22 × 40 cm (9 × 16 in) piece of felt for boot soles

30 cm (12 in) medium weight synthetic wadding [padding], 90 cm (36 in) wide

Sewing thread to match bias strips

Dressmakers' graph paper

TO MAKE THE BOOTS

The boots are quilted and lined with ties at the back and can be worn straight or with turned down cuffs. Quilted felt soles are stitched to uppers with binding which is also sewn round back opening and top edges and forms ties. Fabric for binding should be good quality firm woven cotton, otherwise it will wear out quickly.

Making the pattern

The pattern given fits the foot of a child approximately five years old. Enlarge the pattern pieces from the diagram (**fig. 1**). The boots can be made to fit any size foot.

To make your own pattern, draw round the foot (not too close to leave room for movement).

Mark a centre line and add seam allowance (**fig. 2**). Measure the length of the centre line and transfer it to a second piece of paper. Draw a line at right angles to the end; this marks centre back line of boot and should be the length required for height of boot.

Draw top of boot at right angle to back, measure round leg at this height and mark half of this measurement on top of boot.

Draw front as shown (**fig. 3**).

Make sure to round toe up or boots will feel tight.

Add seam allowance to front and sole edge and add cuff if required. Adjust quantities of materials.

Cutting out the fabrics

From the felt cut four sole pieces.

From the main fabric cut two pairs of main boot pieces.

From the lining fabric cut the same.

From the wadding [padding] cut four main pieces and two sole pieces.

From the 60 cm (24 in) square of cotton cut bias strips 4 cm (1½ in) wide to make two strips each 2.1 m (2⅜ yd) long (adjust according to size).

Quilting the fabric

Mark quilting lines with tailors' chalk on right side of four main fabric pieces and lay these right side up on wadding [padding]. Pin and baste.

With very loose pressure on presser foot, stitch along the quilting lines.

To make the soles, sandwich wadding [padding] between the felt. Baste round edges and, starting in centre of heel, stitch round and round forming a spiral (**fig. 1**). Continue round close to edge of front of sole, and work round forming a spiral finishing at the centre.

To finish

Stitch front seams on main pieces, press seams open and zig-zag stitch over seam line.

Trim seam allowance on curve so that seam lies flat. Join back seams in the same way. Stitch front and back seams on lining. Double stitch on curved parts of front seams and clip seam so it lies flat.

Put lining inside quilting, wrong sides together. Sew top and bottom edges very close to edge.

Pin upper to sole with back and front seams matching centre line of sole. Sew with a large stitch length.

Press bias strips in half lengthways, wrong sides together. Lay raw edges of binding on sole seam of upper. Baste round edge, taking care that binding is not stretched – rather stretch the sole seam very slightly. Overlap ends. Machine stitch. Roll binding onto wrong side and pin folded edge so that it laps over seam line. Machine stitch from upper side of boot, close to sewn edge of binding.

Make ties from bias strips and sew in position on the back seam.

Bind back opening, starting with raw edges on quilted side. Bind top edge in same way as back opening, using extra length of binding to form ties.

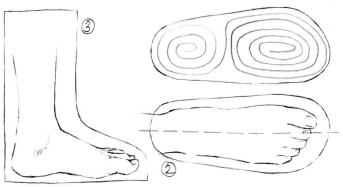

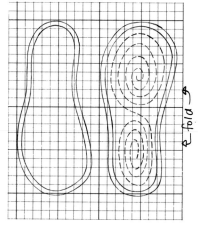

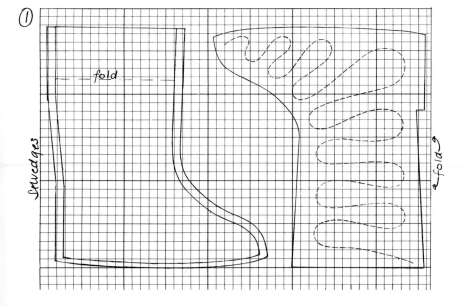

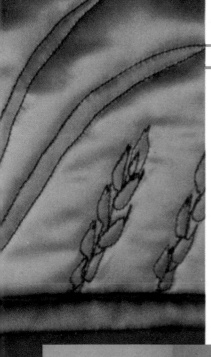

'FIELD OF LIGHT' WALL HANGING

This bold and exciting wall hanging design involves a lot of painstaking work and accurate measurement. Made up in brightly coloured satins in nine different shades, it incorporates patchwork and quilting, hand painting and free machine embroidery. The experienced needlewoman will find it a challenging and rewarding project.

'Field of Light' wall hanging

Finished size: 122 × 152 cm (48 × 60 in)

MATERIALS

25 cm (10 in) white satin, 90 cm (36 in) wide (colour 1)

25 cm (10 in) cream satin, 90 cm (36 in) wide (colour 2)

25 cm (10 in) pale yellow satin, 90 cm (36 in) wide (colour 3)

75 cm (29 in) brilliant yellow satin, 90 cm (36 in) wide (colour 4)

1.5 m (1¾ yd) golden yellow satin, 90 cm (36 in) wide (colour 5)

1 m (39 in) scarlet satin, 90 cm (36 in) wide (colour 6)

75 cm (29 in) emerald green satin, 90 cm (36 in) wide (colour 7)

1 m (39 in) olive green satin, 90 cm (36 in) wide (colour 8)

1.5 m (1¾ yd) bottle green satin, 90 cm (36 in) wide (colour 9)

2.75 m (3 yd) lightweight synthetic wadding [padding], 90 cm (36 in) wide

2.25 m (2½ yd) calico [unbleached cotton] for backing, 183 cm (72 in) wide

Sewing thread to match satin

Green sewing thread for quilting

Paper

22 × 38 cm (9 × 15 in) card [cardboard] for template

Ruler

Coloured pencils

Felt tip marker

Tailors' chalk

Protractor

Mid-green fabric dye (use a permanent, washable dye that can be fixed by pressing)

Paintbrush

TO MAKE THE WALL HANGING

Preparing the design
Borders measure 20 cm (8 in) deep in all.
Central area measures 82 × 112 cm (32 × 44 in).
Draw design full size on paper following the working plan (**fig.**

1). Divide lightly into 30 cm and 15 cm (12 in and 6 in) squares for ease of working and fill in the colour key with coloured pencils. The colours are keyed as follows: 1 white, 2 cream, 3 pale yellow, 4 brilliant yellow, 5 golden yellow, 6 scarlet, 7 emerald green, 8 olive green, 9 bottle green.
Make the template for the central area diagonal strips (**fig. 2**).

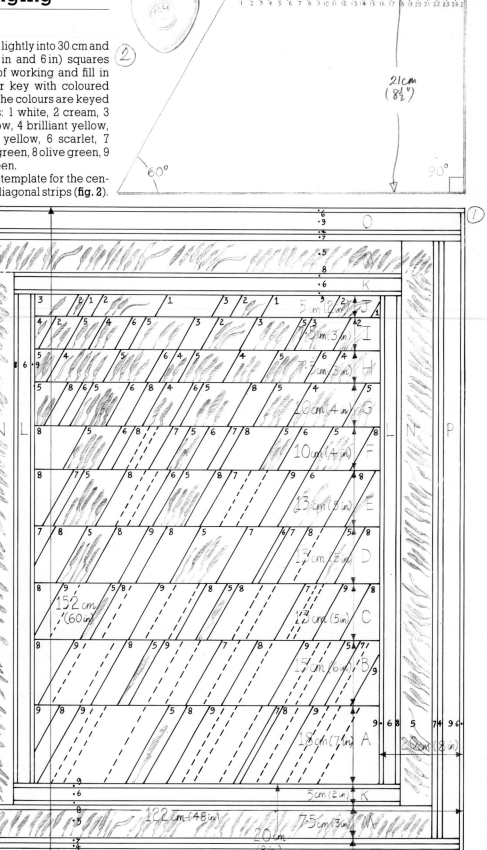

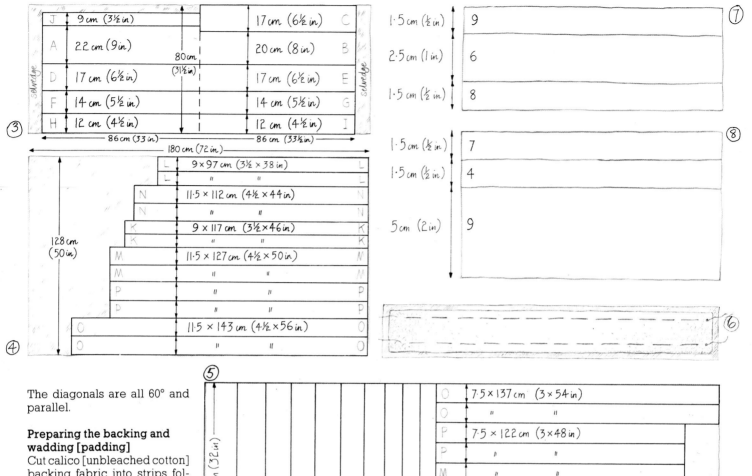

The diagonals are all 60° and parallel.

Preparing the backing and wadding [padding]
Cut calico [unbleached cotton] backing fabric into strips following the layout in **fig. 3** and **fig. 4**. Mark each strip with the appropriate letter as you cut it out using the felt tip marker. Cut the wadding [padding] into strips as shown in the layout diagram (**fig. 5**).
Baste each wadding [padding] strip to its appropriate backing strip using long firm stitches. There will be a 2 cm (¾ in) seam allowance between edge of wadding [padding] and backing (**fig. 6**).
Complete all the strips for both the central area and the border in this way. Put aside.

Preparing the satin borders
Cut out the satin, following the working plan (**fig. 1**). Allow 1.2 cm (½ in) seam allowance all around.
Border strips K and L consist of colours and quantities shown in **fig. 7**.
Strips M and N are made up of colour 5 only (sizes as in **fig. 4**).
Strips O and P consist of colours and quantities shown in **fig. 8**.
To make strips up to the required length, cut them out across the width of the fabric and piece together with a straight seam.
Press seams open.
Cut scarlet satin binding strips for edges as follows: cut two strips 4 × 152 cm (1½ × 60 in); cut two strips 4 × 127 cm (1½ × 50 in).

Preparing the central area
Using the card [cardboard] template (**fig. 2**) against the full size working plan (**fig. 1**), cut out the satin strips for the central area. Add 2 cm (¾ in) seam allowance all around each piece. Use tailors' chalk to draw round template.
Mark out pieces using template as shown in **fig. 9** then add seam allowance.
Cut out all the pieces for each colour at the same time and place them in their approximate positions on the backing strips of calico [unbleached cotton] and wadding [padding]. Pin and set aside.
Paint wheat ear motif on appropriate sections (**fig. 1**) and fix by pressing.

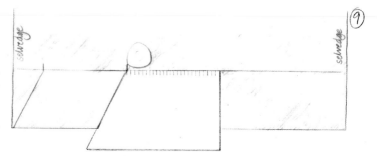

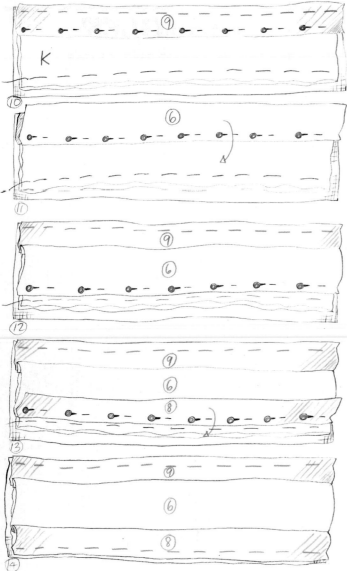

strip. Baste along the edges. Then work the diagonal lines of quilting (broken lines in **fig. 1**) and free machine stitch around the wheat ear motif in green thread.

Complete all sections from A to J in this way.

Join sections together to complete the central panel. With right sides facing, pin and baste, allowing 2 cm ($\frac{3}{4}$ in) for seams. Machine stitch sections together and oversew raw edges with zig-zag or interlock stitch. Join A to B in this way, then C to AB and D to ABC and so on until panel is complete.

Attaching the borders

Sew the border strips to the central panel. Follow the same procedure as that used to join the sections of the central panel together.

Begin by attaching vertical strips L to each side of the central panel. Then join strips

K to top and bottom.

Attach strips N to L at the sides.

Attach strips M to K at top and bottom.

Attach strips P to N at the sides.

Attach strips O to M at top and bottom.

To finish

Pin and baste scarlet satin binding strips to the edges, beginning with the vertical sides. Line up edge of binding with edge of strips P. Machine stitch and fold binding strip over to the back, turn in a hem of 1.2 cm ($\frac{1}{2}$ in) and hem all around on the back of the hanging.

Repeat with binding strips at top and bottom.

Make four loops from scraps of backing fabric and sew to backing at 30 cm (12 in) intervals along top edge of hanging.

Push a wooden or metal rod through these loops to suspend the hanging.

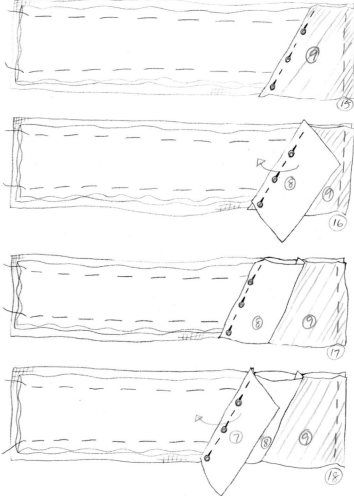

Sewing the borders

Sew the border strips K and L, O and P as shown in **figs. 10** to **14**. Before sewing border strips M and N, paint on the wheat ear design and fix.

Quilting the wheat ear design

Use the darning foot of the sewing machine and lower the feed dog. Use dark green thread and straight stitch freely around the painted design to quilt all the layers together.

The upper tension may need slackening in order to give a rounded stitch on the surface. Pull all thread ends through to the back of the work and tie off. Put all labelled and completed border sections aside while working central panel.

Sewing the central panel

Following the working plan (**fig. 1**), complete each strip, working from the bottom of the panel upwards. Begin with Section A and complete the whole of that strip before moving on to work Section B.

Begin at the right-hand side of Section A, attaching strips of satin as shown in **fig. 15** to **fig. 18**. Baste the first piece of satin (in colour 9) to the backing and wadding [padding]. Pin the left-hand edge of the satin. Then pin the second piece of satin (in colour 8) to colour 9, right sides facing. Machine stitch; lightly press seam flat. Continue sewing the pieces together in this way until you reach the left-hand edge of the

'TRIANGLES' WALL HANGING

The easy-to-follow instructions for this wall hanging may inspire you to make up your own design.
Note how the lines of quilting echo and emphasize the patchwork pattern, and also add texture to the plain fabrics.

'Triangles' wall hanging

Finished size: 120 × 227 cm (48 × 89 in)

MATERIALS

1.5 m (1¾ yd) red fabric, 90 cm (36 in) wide

1.9 m (2⅛ yd) blue fabric, 90 cm (36 in) wide

1.2 m (1⅓ yd) green fabric, 90 cm (36 in) wide

1.5 m (1¾ yd) yellow fabric, 90 cm (36 in) wide

4 m (4½ yd) backing fabric, 90 cm (36 in) wide

46 cm (18 in) green fabric for binding, 90 cm (36 in) wide

4.8 m (5¼ yd) synthetic wadding [padding], 90 cm (36 in) wide

Matching sewing thread in red, blue, green and yellow

Quilting thread in green

Quilting frame longer than 250 cm (98 in) between stretchers or large quilting hoop

Dark coloured pencil for marking light fabrics

Light coloured pencil for marking dark fabrics

Dressmakers' graph paper

Tracing paper in large sheets

Long ruler

TO MAKE THE HANGING

Enlarge each of the seven sections of the working plan (**fig. 1**) and draw them out full size on the dressmakers' graph paper. Label each shape in each section.

The work on each of the seven sections of the design, from making the paper patterns to sewing the fabric pieces together, should be complete before starting on the next section. Once the second section has been completed, it should be sewn to the first before going on to the third.

Sewing the patchwork

The seam allowance throughout is 1 cm (⅜ in). Use the seam guide marked on the throat plate of your sewing machine, or mark your own with masking tape. By feeding the patches

through the machine against the masking tape you will keep an exact seam allowance throughout the work (**fig. 2**).

Lay out the enlarged drawing of Section 1; trace off triangle A accurately. Add 1 cm (⅜ in) seam allowance all around and label the piece. Repeat for shapes B, C, D, and E. Cut out the fabric pieces using the tracings as templates. Leave

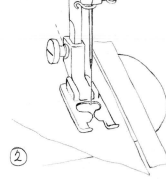

the patterns pinned to the fabric until they are needed for sewing.

Note that shapes labelled 'cut 2' must be cut out mirror fashion.

Sew triangle B to top of shape A; press seams upwards.

Sew the two C shapes to either side of triangle AB; press seams outwards. Note: in this case, do not match the edges, match the seam lines, which will result in the edges being slightly offset; this will occur often (**fig. 3**).

Sew triangle D to the top of shape CABC; press seam upwards.

Sew the two E shapes to either side of triangle CABCD; press seams outwards.

Put Section 1 aside and make Section 2 by the same method, following the working plan (**fig. 1**) carefully.

Sew Sections 1 and 2 together and press seam upwards.

Make up Section 3 and join to the other two sections before making Section 4.

Complete the rest of the patchwork in the same way.

Quilting the fabric

Press the patchwork on the wrong side. Spread it out right side up.

Starting at the top and using the ruler and coloured pencils, lightly mark the quilting lines that follow on from the patchwork seams. Set them in about 3 mm (⅛ in) from the seam line (**fig. 4**). Mark in as many other quilting lines as you want to sew.

Cut the backing fabric into three equal pieces and join them together to make a sheet 132 cm (52 in) wide with two horizontal seams. This sheet will be too long, so cut 12 cm (5 in) off top and bottom. Keep one scrap to make a sleeve to hang the completed wall hanging.

Cut the wadding [padding] in half and make up with one vertical overlapping seam. This will be too wide, so trim 40 cm (16 in) off one side.

The layers must now be basted together. Spread backing out, place wadding [padding] on top and lay the patchwork, right side up, centrally on the wadding [padding]. Pin and

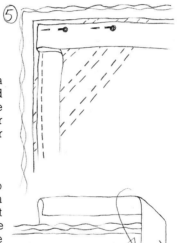

baste the layers together, working from the centre outwards. Put in as many extra lines of basting as you think necessary, particularly if you are not using a frame or hoop. Finally baste all around the edge.

Mount the quilt in a frame or hoop if you have one. The quilting can be done without a frame, provided it is securely basted together and is supported on a table or your knees and a chair. It should not be allowed to hang down to the floor.

Work from the centre outwards. If you are quilting without a frame be careful not to pull the stitches too tight; keep an even tension throughout. Only remove the basting stitches as you quilt if you find them being caught down by the quilting. Do not remove the basting stitches around the edges.

Wherever possible fasten threads off at the quilt edge. For neatness use this method: measure a comfortable length of thread for quilting and double

it. Starting at the apex of a triangle, work half the thread out in one direction, leaving the other end to be picked up later and worked out in the other direction.

Binding the edges

Cut the binding fabric into strips 4 cm (1½ in) wide. Join them into a continuous strip at least 7.1 m (7⅞ yd) long. Loop the binding up loosely and secure with a pin, releasing a little at a time as you work.

Starting at the bottom left-hand side, pin the binding through all the layers, matching up the edge of the binding to the edge of the patchwork. Pin up to the first corner.

The first step in mitring the corner is to fold the binding up squarely from the corner,

pinch it to mark a crease and put a pin in along the crease.

Stitch through all the layers starting 12 cm (5 in) from the bottom corner and 1 cm (⅜ in) from the edge. Sew up to the crease and fasten off.

Continue the mitre by folding the binding up along the existing crease and down again to lie along the top edge (**fig. 5**).

Pin the binding along the top edge and mitre second corner. Continue until last corner has been mitred. However, before sewing the remainder of the binding down, the two ends

must be joined. A diagonal seam is best, but more difficult than a straight one.

Remove all basting and fasten off any thread ends. Trim excess backing and wadding [padding] to the edge of the patchwork. Turn binding over to the back of the work, turn under a hem and bring it down to meet the line of machining. Pin and hem in place.

On reaching the corner, fold the binding to complete the mitre (**figs. 6** and **7**).

To hang the wall hanging

Take the 12 cm (5 in) scrap from the backing fabric, trim it to the exact width of the hanging. Fold in half lengthwise, right sides together and seam along one edge and down one end (**fig. 8**). Turn right side out, turn raw edge in and stitch end closed. Pin and baste sleeve to top of hanging; hem top and bottom edges of sleeve to the backing. The sleeve can now be used to take a wooden or metal rod and will not show on the right side of the hanging (**fig. 9**).

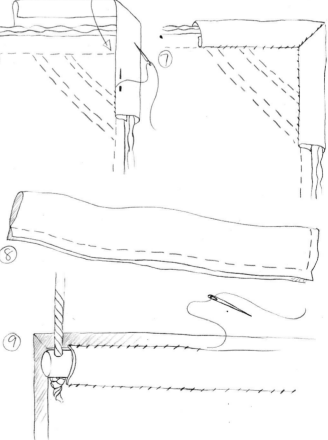

WOODLAND PANEL

The instructions for this beautiful woodland scene show you how to build up a three-dimensional panel by working with layers of felt, wadding and fabric.
The process of piecing together such a complex design takes time and patience but is well worth the effort.

Finished size: 50 × 64 cm (20 × 25 in)

MATERIALS

Dupion curtain fabric [shiny finish drapery fabric], 90 cm (36 in) wide:

40 cm (16 in) each 2 shades green (fabrics A and B)

15 cm (6 in) each 2 further shades of green (fabrics C and D)

20 cm (8 in) beige (fabric G)

2 small pieces green velvet (fabrics E and F)

2 m (2¼ yd) synthetic wadding [padding], 90 cm (36 in) wide

30 cm (12 in) square of felt

76 × 89 cm (30 × 35 in) piece of calico [unbleached cotton]

Embroidery wools, stranded embroidery thread and pearl cotton in shades of green and beige

Quilting wool or thick knitting wool

Tapestry needle

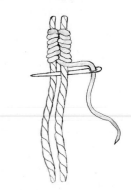

⑤

7 m (7½ yd) piping cord

50 × 64 cm (20 × 25 in) hardboard

Fine string (for mounting)

50 × 64 cm (20 × 25 in) sheet of paper

Tissue paper

Tracing paper

Pencil

TO MAKE THE PANEL

Enlarge complete working plan of panel (**fig. 1**) to full size. Using tissue paper, trace the shapes in **fig. 2**. Pin tissue to calico [unbleached cotton] and baste through paper and fabric along the lines of the design. Tear away paper leaving design outlined in stitches.
Trace central G section of design (**fig. 2**) on tissue, add 2 cm (¾ in) turning allowance. Place on fabric G, baste through and tear away paper as before.
Cut felt shapes (**fig. 3**) and hem stitch in position on calico [unbleached cotton] backing. Place fabric G in position on backing and outline tree trunks and foliage shapes in back stitch.

①

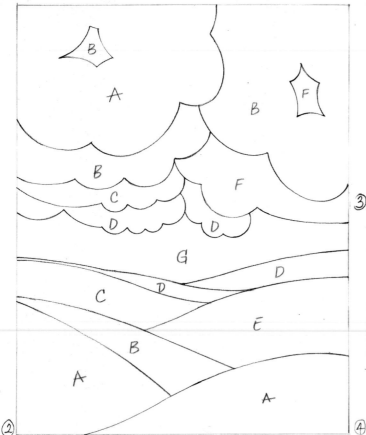

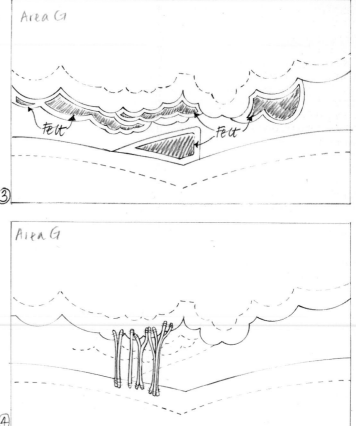

Using a needle without a point, thread quilting wool between felt and fabric G to pad out the form of the tree trunks (see Italian quilting).

Sew pieces of piping cord in position (**fig. 4**) and, using pearl cotton, weave cords together (**fig. 5**, page 75).

On tracing paper, draw foliage shapes (**fig. 6**), adding a 2 cm (¾ in) seam allowance as before. Cut felt shapes and sew to background.

Take fabric D and cut to shape, adding extra fabric all round to cover padding. Pin or baste in place over felt padding and machine stitch in place using straight stitch.

Trim fabric close to stitching (**fig. 7**). Stitch around piece again using wide zig-zag stitch and short stitch length (**fig. 8**).

Make some narrow tubes, or rouleau, from the remaining scraps of fabric (**fig. 9**); thread with cords to use for larger tree trunks. Add the tree trunks to this completed section.

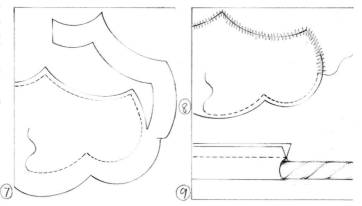

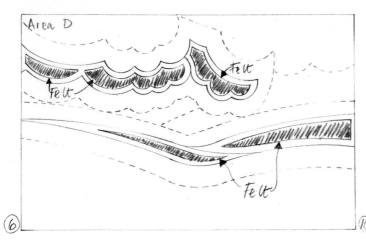

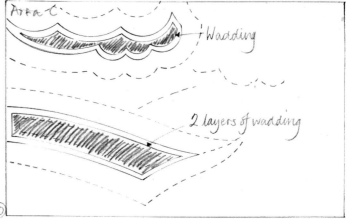

Make patterns and apply wadding [padding] layers as in **fig. 10**. When more than one layer of wadding [padding] is used sew smaller pieces on first.

Using patterns, cut shapes from fabric C. The embroidery on the bank must be worked by hand before this section is sewn to the panel.

The stitches used for this panel were as follows: French knots in pearl cotton for flowers; bullion knots in three strands of embroidery thread; straight stitches using one strand.

Machine stitch fabric to panel as before. Add large tree trunk using cord and rouleau.

Make patterns and apply wadding [padding] layers as in **fig. 12**.

Cut the bank from fabric E; machine stitch in place as before. Add the tree trunk, pulling cords through fabric E, using **fig. 1** as a guide, and complete the needleweaving.

Cut out foliage shapes and peep-through section in fabric F. Machine stitch in place.

Add the other tree trunk using cords and rouleau. Weave the cord together, leaving some of the rouleau uncovered.

Add cords to peep-through section, and bind with thread or wool.

Make patterns and apply layers of wadding [padding] as in **fig. 13**. Cut shapes from fabric B and work embroidery. Machine stitch pieces in position over wadding [padding]; add second peep-through section. Add tree trunk, using rouleau and some cord. Add cords to peep-through section and bind with thread or wool.

Make patterns and apply wadding [padding] as in **fig. 14**. Cut shapes from fabric A.

Machine stitch pieces over wadding [padding]. Add remaining tree trunk in cords, pulling cords through bank.

To mount the panel

Place hardboard behind panel, turning surplus fabric over. Using the fine string, lace the fabric together along the two long sides, draw tight and fasten off. Repeat along two shorter sides. The panel is now ready to frame.

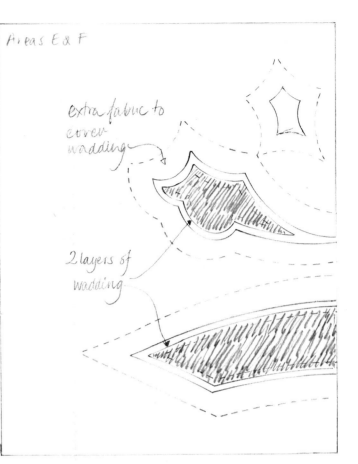

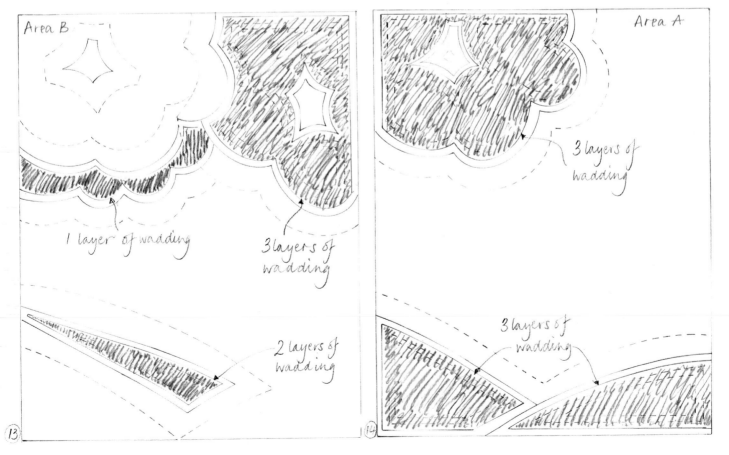

Quilting Supplies

UNITED KINGDOM

The following sell a wide selection of fabrics, sewing accessories and quilting materials.

John Lewis & Co Ltd
Oxford Street
London W1A 1EX
Tel: 01-629 7711

McCullock & Wallis Ltd
25–26 Dering Street
London W1R 0BH
Tel: 01-629 0311

Mace & Nairn
89 Crane Street
Salisbury
Wiltshire
Tel: Salisbury 6903

Christine Riley
53 Barclay Street
Stonehaven
Kincardineshire AB3 2AR
Tel: Stonehaven 3238

The following sell quilting supplies by mail order:

Strawberry Fayre
Stockbridge
Hants SO20 6HF
Fine American cotton fabrics, waddings, hoops and threads (send s.a.e. for details)

The Patchwork Dog & The Calico Cat
21 Chalk Farm Road
London NW1
Fabrics, waddings, hoops, threads and quilt kits (send s.a.e. for details)

The Quiltery
Tacolneston
Norwich
Norfolk
NR16 1DW
Templates and quilt kits (send s.a.e. for details)

Quad Quilts
Elvendon Road
Goring-on-Thames
RG8 0LP
Quilt kits (send s.a.e. for details)

The Silver Thimble
33 Gay Street
Bath
Avon BA1 2NT
Templates and other quilting supplies (send A5 s.a.e. for details)

UNITED STATES

The following nationwide chain stores usually stock a wide selection of quilting supplies: Ben Franklin Stores; Jefferson Stores; Kay Mart; M H Lamston; The May Co; Neisners; J C Penney Stores; Sears Roebuck; Two Guys and Woolworth's.

The following sell quilting supplies by mail order:

American Handicrafts
2617 W Seventh Street
Fort Worth, Texas 76707
All craft supplies

The Counting House at the Hammock Shop
Box 155
Pawleys Island,
So Carolina 29585
Materials, threads, hoops, needles and frames

Economy Handicrafts
50–21 69th Street
Woodside, New York 11377
All craft supplies

W Houst & Sons
Woodstock, New York 12498
Quilting threads

Lee Wards
Elgin, Illinois 60120
All craft supplies

Peters Valley Craftsmen
Layton, New Jersey 07851
All craft supplies

The Stearns & Foster Co
P O Box 15380
Cincinnati, Ohio 45215
Batting, frames and all quilting supplies

INDEX